TIME, TRIALS, AND TRIUMPHS

Julie C. Weidner

TIME,
TRIALS,
AND
TRIUMPHS

Julie C. Weidner
Boone, NC 28607

Print ISBN: 9798627795249
Imprint: Independently published

Printed in the United States of America on SFI Certified paper.
First Edition

Dedication

I would like to dedicate this book to everyone who has supported me in the last couple of years, especially my friends Christina and Melissa. This book is being launched on Melissa's birthday. Happy Birthday, Melissa.

Without my dearest friends: Melissa, Christina, Douglas, Deniece, Wanda, Mamma Liz, Merrilee, Bonnie, Audrey, my Editor Anita Laymon, my church, and Sunday School class, as well as a few other friends, this book would not have come to light. I truly thank you from the bottom of my heart.

Also, I would like to thank the two friends who had helped me to proof my wording and grammar mistakes before I turned my script over to Anita for editing. They are my dear friends Shelly Campbell (Teacher), and Bill Imperatore (Professor Emeritus). Thank you so very much for your help in this writing process.

Thank you to my Mom, Sara, and my second adopted Mom, Ruth. Without the two of you, I would not have made it through my youth.

Thank you Christina, for all you do for me! Thank you for giving me ideas to write about, and for encouraging me to keep on living through years of suicidal thoughts and behaviors. Your love saw me through these times and let me know that I was loved.

Thank you, Melissa, for your encouragement especially. I have written an enormous amount of essays on what I have learned from you and the influence that you have made in my life. Many of the things I have written will be for my eyes only, but I have shared several things in this book. Without your support and words, "You Got This!", I would never have even had the courage to allow myself to be vulnerable enough to put myself Out-There so daringly.

My Dear Friends

'Book Dedication Poem'

My friends kept me going.
They are the spine that kept me alive.
With prayers they constantly
Surrounded me,
And kept Jesus
By my side.
In the darkest despair
Of hallucinations,
My friends never ran away.
Instead, they contacted me
To support and Love me
Every single day.
I dedicate this book to them,
Because I know without their support,
My dreams of becoming a published author
Would never have come true and forth.
They saw me come from the darkness
Of mental illness
To the Light of the Lord.
They celebrated my Baptism,
And aided in my victory over
Hardships, family troubles, mental illness,
And over the negative way I saw myself.
My Dear Friends and Jesus,
This VICTORY is yours!
I Love you, My Dear Friends!

Acknowledgements

I would like to thank the following people for their love, hard work, and moral support:

Jesus Christ, first and foremost, for dying on the infamous cross for me and loving me when the world, including myself, rejected me.

Melissa F. Gragg, for her encouragement and for kicking me into gear to work on getting my writing published and for believing in me when I did not believe in myself. She always had my back and when I would get to a panic point, she would tell me that "You got this!" Melissa, We have 'got this' together.

Christina M. Carver, for staying up on the phone with me on late nights when I wanted to throw in the towel on life both figuratively and realistically. She never let me just give in. Also, for following Melissa's lead and kicking me into gear to publish. You helped me to find the courage to expose some of my inner thoughts to this dark world, hopefully to add some light to it by sharing my victory.

Anita Laymon, for being my editor when I could not afford to pay her and for teaching me a lot about the writing and editing process. She has become a dear friend of mine. Anita has done all the publishing hard work for me.

Douglas Hunt, my little (younger), big (taller) adopted brother, for his encouragement to keep writing over the years when I wanted to give up on writing and communicating altogether. Douglas is a huge part of my support system.

Shelly Campbell, for being a special support and for helping to edit my spelling and grammar mistakes before this book went to Anita.

Shelly you are terrific, and I LOVE you so dearly. Give John a big hug for me and when you do that's a hug from me too.

Bill Imperatore, for his support and hard work at helping me not only get my mistakes corrected, but also for his advice on how to better get my point across to let the reader better understand my work. He also helped me to decide what to put into this book and what to leave out of it.

Sara Weidner, my Mom, for being there when the rest of our family wasn't, for giving birth to me, and for fighting for me to stay in my own apartment when the mental health system, my dad, and courts wanted to institutionalize me.

Ruth Batcheler, for taking me in when I was a young woman. She was an angel who took me off the streets from being homeless to give me shelter, food, and clothing expecting nothing else in return. She loved me and still loves me, unconditionally.

Kim Hill, my former peer support counselor, for supporting and encouraging me to follow through with my dream of becoming a published author. The same goes to my IPS counselors, James Lawson and Michelle Young.

Terri Cleavinger, my Vocational Rehabilitation counselor, for helping to find resources to learn how to navigate a computer and how to use a word processor.

Pastor Todd Houston, his wife Alisha, and my Sunday School Class at Mount Vernon Baptist Church in Boone, North Carolina for always keeping me in their prayers. These prayers brought me to Jesus. They are the most loving and supportive people in the world.

I also acknowledge the MVBC staff and congregation for their prayers when I was struggling and for praying me to the Lord when I felt that even Jesus would not accept me. When I felt so very unlovable, they loved me anyway.

Grandma Scheschi, for making me promise to her, before she died, that I would publish some of my writings.

Bonnie and Merrilee, the other two-thirds of us three musketeers from Holly Hill Hospital. They spent countless hours on the phone listening to what I wrote and would tell me if it was good or not. If my work did not pass their test, it would not pass the test of any other reader. They, along with another friend, Audrey, understood me when no one else did.

My mental health providers, Dr. Hoover-Thompson and Miranda Schooley, my therapists, for working with me through the difficult times of being suicidal, disassociation spells that would send me to the emergency room, and through an eating disorder. They are more than just counselors to me, they are also friends.

Life Coaches Nicole Klett and Janet Puza-Dillin, for giving me life lessons to learn about and to write about. When Nicole left her job, I thought that I was toast, but Janet has done a great job in taking her place. They are both uplifting people.

My CCNC Nurse Care Manager, Marcella Bradford, for talking to me every Monday and being an influence on my work. Her support is phenomenal.

My Vaya Health Mental Health case manager, Stephanie Jessaph, for taking up the slack of my other support systems when they were not available.

Contents

Prologue

I am sitting in Melissa's informal dining room enjoying the country-cottage feel of her home; just finishing watching some Brené Brown videos. The videos made me both laugh hard and think even harder than I laughed. I guess that's what they were meant to do. Brené is a Social Worker who studies courage and vulnerability.

Brené said in one of her videos, **"True belonging doesn't require you to change who you are, it requires you to be who you are."**[1] As Brené was saying this, I realized that I had not belonged or had any sense of belonging until the last two to three years of my life, and I'm fifty-two years old. Watching Melissa live and accept herself in a way I had never seen anyone model this kind of self-acceptance before has taught me how to belong to myself. In doing so, I have a sense of belonging in the social systems that I surround myself in and with, and I feel accepted in the community around me.

I even feel, or understand more, the power of belonging that Jesus has given and extended to each of us, particularly to me. For so much of my life, darkness has ruled over it through suicidal feelings, mania, PTSD, schizophrenia, depression, self-doubt, and self-talk. Jesus took these things in my life and made them manageable. He gave me the ability to write about what I experience and what I feel. I believe that Jesus did not remove them from me entirely because of my ability to communicate

---

[1] https://loud-silent.com/

with the outside world and express to the world from an inside view what these types of mental illnesses are like from an inside perspective. By doing this, He is allowing me to possibly help someone else who finds a family member in my shoes or someone who is experiencing these types of mental illnesses themselves.

As one of my therapists told me, "most people with schizophrenia are so locked inside their own world of hallucinations and delusions that they do not possess the ability to articulate what they are experiencing, thinking, and/or how they are feeling." I too have experienced this. I was lucky and found a doctor years ago who was able to medicate me to the point that I became lucid and able to communicate most of the time and now pretty much all of the time. I wish she were still my doctor, but the agency went belly-up and a new organization took over. She left and went to work for Appalachian State University, I believe.

I've had some okay doctors, competent doctors, and some not-so-okay doctors since, but the doctor that I really owe my current stability to is the one who put me on Invega Sustenna. It's a monthly injection used for treating schizophrenia. I've had so many different doctors. With doctors coming and going in the mental health system where I live, I do not remember which doctor put me on this injection. I have found Invega Sustenna to be a life-changer for me because it has pretty much cleared my thoughts. With clear thoughts now going through my head, I have dared to do and attempt things that I had only the audacity to dream about previously.

I attempted to go back to school, taking online courses at Grand Canyon University in January 2019, only to have a head injury during a face-planting on the floor during a seizure at the doctor's office. I was not cleared medically to go back to school. For now, or at least as of this time, my medical doctor wants me to wait until I am released by my psychologist before he will sign papers allowing me to return to studying. Dr. Thompson and I talked about it. We decided that I need to get my disassociation spells under control before I return, as they are what leads to the seizure episodes. She feels this could take a year or so. I have decided in the meantime to take the time to work extremely hard on my recovery and on a writing career; writing stories, essays, poems, or whatever comes to mind. I like to call them *worded-picture-clips*.

Brené Brown would be proud, as I am all in! I have put myself out there, and on May 7, 2020, my first book will be launched. Succeed? Fail? It's all relevant. I'm allowing myself to be vulnerable on a global level. Brené says, "Vulnerability is the breakdown or core of shame and fear and our struggle for worthiness." She could not have gotten that one more right, as through almost all my life, I have felt so unworthy. I made the fast-pitch team because my dad was the coach, mind you. I earned my starting position and did NOT bench. I was told that I was good with children because that was the family business. I got sick with schizophrenia, and was on disability to support myself, as I couldn't function well enough to stay out of the hospital, even without a job. Writing has given me more courage, freedom, self-respect, a sense of belonging, and worthiness that I have not found otherwise. Finally, I Believe I'm Enough! I feel comfortable in my own skin living for myself, not for others to walk all over me.

Brené quoted a 1910 Theodore Roosevelt speech: "It's not the critic that counts. It's not the man who points out how the strong man stumbles or when the doer of deeds could have done it differently. The credit actually belongs to the man who strives valiantly, who errors, and comes up short again, and again, and again. Who in the end, while he may know the triumph of high achievement, at least when he fails, he does so daringly." [2]

I can honestly say that in the past six months, I have lived and strived more valiantly and dared to fail more daringly than ever in my lifetime. In doing so I have both fallen flat on my face and I have succeeded to heights I never could have imagined before.

Through Brené Brown, I have learned that I have found a light inside myself through the beauty of my vulnerability. I have discovered that I do have the courage that my friends and mental health team have been telling me all along that I have. I find this courage in my faith in Jesus. I find that the light that exists within myself is exceptionally dim compared to "the Light" that I found in Him. It is His Light through me that keeps me going

---

[2] https://hiplatina.com/brene-brown-netflix-special-mental-helth-month

and is what has given me the courage to write once again.

I depend on Jesus' strength to write and be able to expose myself in such a vulnerable way.

Julie Weidner

Today

Today's the day I start again,
Fearless ~ I have overcome.
Today's the day that I define myself
By the battles that I have won.
Today's the day I say to you, my friends:
"Thank you for your help."
Because of it, I have lots to gain.
And a spirit to overcome.
Today's the day there's a child in me,
One who has lots to learn.
The fantasies of this child,
Marvels at every turn.
Today's the day, I grow up inside
And set healthy boundaries for my life.
Today, I will make healthy decisions
For my life
That will turn the test of time…

-- -- -- -- -- ❧ -- -- -- -- --

Inside My Savior's Gracious Heart and Soul

If I could put my fears in a box,
Just how big would it have to be?
Because these fears so often consume
Every square inch of me…

If all my fears fit in a box,
How could I guess how much it would weigh?
It would be an enormous box
Guessing by how heavy it would be
If my mind, heart, and soul
Were to be the gauge.

Would a mountain range
With its peaks and valleys,
Be enough to hold
The tears that have paralyzed
Both my heart and soul?
Would a major river that empties
Into an ocean even be able
To contain the floods inside my soul?

The only box that is big enough,
Isn't a box at all!
It is found inside the Love and Light
Of my Savior's gracious heart and soul!

-- -- -- -- -- ❧ -- -- -- -- --

Standing Tall

In the guest room that I sleep in at Melissa's house, she has a bear carved out of wood with a chainsaw. The bear stands on its hind legs in an erect position, as if curious, defensive, or dancing. Every time I look at this bear, it reminds me to Stand Tall like Melissa and Christina do. It also reminds me to fight for what I believe in, to work for happiness, and to always be forthright and honest.

Now, what is it that I stand for? I believe in the basic rights that we are given as American citizens: life, liberty, and the pursuit of happiness. But, not at the expense of another person's rights. I also believe that every human being deserves food, clean water, shelter, and medical care and attention. I believe in the right to privacy, and independent living. I believe that every living creature has the right to live without being bullied or abused in any way, shape, or form.

I will fight for these rights, along with my right make to my own choices. If I become incapacitated, I have had arrangements made for someone that I truly trust to be Power of Attorney. That was a choice and a decision that I can live with and mine to make.

Standing Tall, is about honor, decency, honesty, and fighting for what is right and virtuous. It is having the courage to do the right thing even when it means swimming upstream against the current, and against the crowd.

-- -- -- -- -- ✺ -- -- -- -- --

If you live honestly and honorably, then you can Stand Tall with your head held up high because you have honored not only yourself, but also Abba Father, Most High.

-- -- -- -- -- ❧ -- -- -- -- --

A Perfect Life

If life were perfect, how would it look?
For this to be written out on paper,
One could/can write a book.
Yes, arguments and disagreements may happen,
But, only once in a great, great while.
Then when they happened, the parties involved
Would always work it out…
No guns, no wars,
No murders would ever occur.
No violence in any way!
No rapes would ever happen, nor child abuse,
Children would never be molested, put down,
Or know any abuse.
No one would go hungry, be homeless, bullied,
Beaten, abused, or hurt.
No broken hearts would ever occur!
No one would have to live with blindness,
Being deaf, or as an amputee.
Cancer would have a cure!
No wheelchairs would ever be in need,
There would be an end to all disease!
No more mental illness, or drug abuse,
No alcohol or substance use.
Gender would not determine pay scales,
Amount of labor, or of hours worked.
Men and women would all be treated
As equals in the labor force.
Ethnicity would be treated the same,
For if you look to God, we are all created in His image,

-- -- -- -- -- ☙ -- -- -- -- --

Therefore, we are all the same…
Disability would not even exist.
Cats and dogs would be able to communicate with us.
Humans and animals would coexist
Without allergies or any kind of fear.
The rainbow would still have all its colors in place,
Only there would be no shades of gray.
All decisions would be black or white,
And only honesty would lead the way.
Children would never have to grow-up,
And grownups can be as a child.
All getting along and playing constantly.
Clapping and laughing,
Now would that not be wild?
Spaceships would travel the galaxies
In only minutes at a time…
Moms, dads, and others
Would never get high on drugs,
Or drunk on wine.
Gambling would never have existed at all…
Nor would guns, dope, tobacco, fights,
Or loss of hope.
All along life's journey,
We would tell lots of jokes…
Playgrounds would be our work and job.
We would never need to sleep or rest.
Fear would never have existed at all…
Nor would have broken hearts, bones, toys, and
dreams…
Kittens would stay small, puffy, and playful.

-- -- -- -- -- ✑ -- -- -- -- --

Puppies would stay clumsy, cute, and loveable…
Now would this not be a pleasant
And a perfect world?
Flowers will always bloom in colors bright,
And the grass will always be green.
At least it would be this way for me.
Right now, I have Hanna-Marie, the words I write…
Plus, I now have
Melissa, Christina, and Deneice,
Along with some other friends
Walking beside me, too.
They are all many blessings that I have right now,
My Jesus, I include you!
I think that in my life
God has blessed me with riches that are
Not worth money.
No, they are worth much…, much… More than that.
It's worth all the riches eternity has to offer; and yet,
So much more than that!
But the perfect life is where we live as Jesus' example,
And Love each other as Jesus LOVES!

About The Author

Julie Weidner and Hydi Ann Marie

My name is Julie Weidner; I live in Boone, North Carolina. I was born November 4th of 1967, in Montgomery, Alabama, into an Air Force family at Maxwell Air Force Base. I really could not say that I am from any one place until I settled in the mountains of Boone, North Carolina, in 1993, just before their worst winter in generations. In my youth, I lived in Ramstein, Germany, and traveled throughout Europe. This time proved to be the epitome of my childhood, as well as a very educational experience for me.

Even during my childhood, I had shown signs of schizoid-behaviors, I did not play with real children. Actually, I thought that they were monsters and that my real friends were imaginary creatures. I would run away

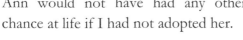

from events and birthday parties that my peers would have. I hid behind bushes or in nearby neighborhoods in backyards for hours until nightfall to ensure everyone was gone before I would come out to be found. Parties involving other children and school terrified me because I was surrounded by what I thought were monsters.

I did not come out of my shell until we moved to Ramstein. We lived in a couple of other villages and towns in Germany before Ramstein; but it was the same as my early childhood. When we moved to Ramstein, I tried out for softball when I was ten and found out that I was a natural athlete.

My first softball team, "The Cardinals," supported me in coming out of my shell and relinquishing the fears I had of people my own age. I made the varsity team in the seventh grade at the young age of twelve. The game season started when I was thirteen. I still proudly display my highly decorated varsity jacket in my home.

Currently, I live with a very loved (some of my friends say "SPOILED!") four-legged friend, Hydi-Ann Marie. I adopted Hydi-Ann on Maundy Thursday, 2014, almost three years after my other cat, Miranda Mae passed in 2011. Both cats were rescues who needed someone to love them, and both cats were special needs cats. Hydi-Ann would not have had any other chance at life if I had not adopted her.

-- -- -- -- -- ✧ -- -- -- -- --

The things that I love to do most of all are: spend quality time with my friends, both the two and four-legged varieties; write; cook and bake (making up my own recipes or tweaking someone else's). There is not much else to tell about myself except that I have been sick most of my adult life.

Returning to my writing as a career and going to school has been a longtime dream of mine. I am returning to writing for others despite what many have told me would never happen in my lifetime, because of communication problems that I have because of the schizophrenia. Schizophrenia is a cruel disease from which I almost did not recover, almost causing my dreams not to come true. The schizophrenia and other disorders that I am recovering from are now being managed through therapy and medications.

School is still on the back burner, although I have enjoyed just getting started in some writing projects again. Academia has been an illusion for me, a dream so many had told me would never come to reality because of the schizophrenia. I have longed to do something with my life, I never really thought about advancing into a life of productivity, just the continuation in my illness. I have fought hard with the help of those in my supportive circle to come out of the dark abyss of confusion and the lack of ability to communicate with the outside world.

I want to relish every academic and progressive day. I love taking in the educational environment that comes

-- -- -- -- -- ❧ -- -- -- -- --

with writing. I do feel that even though I am not in school, as an active writer, I am participating in an academic setting with all the research and learning that goes along with one's writing experiences. Victory, for me, is just being inside of my writing and/or learning environments and relishing in the freedoms I find within them.

I began to write again to show others and myself that despite having disabilities most consider too difficult or challenging to overcome, one can rise above the challenges and make their dreams come true no matter the difficulties. By becoming a published author, I think that if I put my mind to it, I can help others through these challenges— using each of these challenges as a stepping-stone to gain strength, to learn from, and to keep our faith. I will never give up, because the struggle is worth the effort. I will teach those I work with, writing about how I struggled to survive and won.

At publication, I will have a sense of satisfaction that I have completed a step in my life's journey, but I have also proven all the naysayers wrong! I will say to myself what my good friend Melissa has been telling me all along; "You Got This!" Then I will immediately start on another book or enter school, with Melissa and her words behind me all the way. I am working on a second book as I am writing this book, in fact. It's a memoir about my wellness journey and titled, *The Chaos Within.*

After getting my work recognized, I will work toward my goal of reaching out to help others whose dreams were stripped from them. I Will Rise Above My Challenges because, for me, my academic and writing experiences are a step in my recovery process. Having this ability to write has given me a voice that I do not have when it comes to speaking. A sheet of paper opens the door to the world for me, and I plan to step through it.

Helping others through their challenges will help me heal the rest of the way. Forgiving my past abusers will be more comfortable for me as I help others forgive those in their lives who have harmed them, and we will all be better for it. Growth, gain, and fresh, emotional perspective on life is what I hope to teach and to learn as I work in my career as an author working with people who have trauma backgrounds, or who have broken dreams.

My faith has kept me going these past few years. I always knew that I would one day return to the workforce, and my writing is allowing me to be productive. My faith in Jesus Christ kept this dream alive in me. God has blessed me very much in my endeavors as a writer! I know that He has not brought me this far to let me down now, but to lead me on to inspire others to reach their potential and their dreams by being inspired by my story.

I was diagnosed with schizophrenia when I was sixteen years old after my first suicide attempt. The diagnosis was confirmed when I was eighteen years old, and I was hospitalized for an extended period. Truth be told, I was ill with the disability long before I was diagnosed. My birth family was not particularly supportive of me, and it felt like I had become contagious to them.

-- -- -- -- -- ✑ -- -- -- -- --

I felt a lot of anger around me in the environment that I grew up in. I really did not feel much love except when

I excelled in sports, and then, unless I made a mental mistake while playing games, I could do no wrong. I received my varsity letter in the seventh grade for fast-pitch softball. My dad was the coach of the team, and he was a much better coach to me than he was a father. He was, however, a good coach.

I went to school for a forestry degree, which I did not complete, because I turned around and chose to go into the family business of childcare and went after an early childhood education degree with a concentration in literature and journalism. I received my associate degree at Wayne Community College in Goldsboro, North Carolina, and transferred to Appalachian State University in Boone, North Carolina. I got severely sick with schizophrenia before completing my bachelor's degree and had to leave college.

In this collection of poetry, some of the poems were written as early as the eighth grade, but many are current. I have written several while I was in the process of putting this book together just days before turning it over to my editor, Anita Laymon.

-- -- -- -- -- ✑ -- -- -- -- --

Dear Lord,

Help me,

When I am fearful, lost, worried, dismayed, or discontented, to seek your infinite wisdom, courage, perspective, and grace!

In every circumstance and situation, Lord, help me to trust You in my life to guard my thoughts, feelings, and words. Let me trust You to guide me, protect me, and lead me, Lord, so that I may do Your will for my life.

May I end each new day as I start it: serving the Blessed Savior that I so dearly love, Lord. Please help me to remain steadfast in Your will for my life and to reach those that I may come across who do not personally know You as their Father, Lord, and Protector.

In Your Grace and Guidance, Amen

-- -- -- -- -- ✍ -- -- -- -- --

About Pointing A Finger

A few places in this book refer to times when I was abused. Not wanting to be known as a person who points a finger, I purposely did not mention who was toxic or had done the abusing. I have always been told that when one points a finger towards someone else, you have three fingers pointing back at yourself and one pointing up at God. I feel no pleasure out of what had happened to me, and I wish no judgment on those who have harmed me. The only reason I am publishing these poems or essays is to illustrate what life was like for me. I have forgiven the offenders. If they feel I have revealed too much, then that is on them, as I have not disclosed who they are, only the effects these things have had on my life.

I really try living my life by forgiving others, although at times, I do struggle with this and have with my abusers for many years. I was miserable before I learned how to forgive others and to let it all go. Forgiving does not mean forgetting. I believe that these things have happened to me for a reason: to mold, create, and fashion me into the person that I am. I found that God was wise in calling us to forgive each other and have learned that forgiveness isn't to let the other person off the hook, but to give ourselves peace within our heart and soul so that we can live in harmony with the world around us.

-- -- -- -- -- ❧ -- -- -- -- --

This Is Schizophrenia

I really do not know much about a silent world, just what I have gathered from bits and pieces of my experiences of it. I'm basing my experience of a so-called healthy or stable existence from what little of it I have had. To explain my experience of mental illness and schizophrenia, I will first describe what I have experienced in a regular or so-called normal world where things are not scrambled, confused, dark, depressed, hopeless, loud, angered, or high, tornadic, lost, or otherwise unstable.

In my stable world, the first time I went more than a day with no voices, the silence was LOUD and DEAFENING! Quiet times are tough for me because they are not my base point. I have learned to enjoy the times where it is soft, but I do not relish in those times. I relish in the times where conversations are going on all the time, but I am the only one who hears these conversations, just when they are pleasant and routine. I call this "background noise."

Most people, as I understand it, hear traffic: people talking down the hallways, sirens, street noises, music, T.V., radio talk shows, or street traffic. My experience is just as reasonable to me, only it's more pronounced and personalized. Also, my traffic seldom stops.

Healthy is looking at a tree and not seeing a face talking to me, a body pulling its rooting out of the ground so that it can move in some way or even dance. It's sitting in the living-room and not worrying that the walls are

-- -- -- -- -- ✄ -- -- -- -- --

going to fall because they are angry at you, or that the electronics are not conspiring against you to send you away or to spy on what you are doing and on who is with you. Healthy is looking at a rainbow and being wrapped in its wonder and beauty. It's enjoying the inquisitive nature of a child or pet and nurturing that quality in them. Normal is realizing that the simple things are really the essential earthshaking events that one holds onto for life! Those things one would never trade for all the gold in the world. Sane goes beyond plain flavored ice cream and has discovered the hundreds of other flavors and goodness that each share.

Quiet times are challenging for me because they are not my base point. Most of the time -- even when I am asleep, I hear noises: conversations, commands, murmurings, scratchings -- sometimes demonic, sometimes happy, pretty much up and down with the command hallucinations. The command hallucinations were something toward me, not always negative things, or harmful, and never to hurt another person, place, or animal.

Now, I will squash a mosquito, fly, or spider, kill a mouse or snake, but that is as high on the Richter scale as it gets for me when it comes to violence towards other things and entities. I feel guilty just doing this to mosquitos, flies, mice, and snakes. The unruly echoes in my head would haunt me if I were to do this to others, or to pets, livestock, or game meat! I am sure it is much the same way with most of us who have mental illnesses, despite what the press has to say.

-- -- -- -- -- ❧ -- -- -- -- --

On a good day, I wake up on time; I'm able to shower without being in a rush. I take my meds, play with (Hydi-Ann) Hanna Marie, and if it's a perfect day, I will eat breakfast; otherwise, I will go wait outside for the Appalcart (the local bus system) to pick me up for my appointments. When I am finished with my day, I will come home to relax, play some music, write some, and fall asleep if Miss (Hydi-Ann) Hanna Marie does not do her job and keep me awake until ten or eleven PM, (not that I would have slept much at night anyway).

The SIMPLE THINGS! That's what stability, mental wellness, a regular life, "NORMAL," comes from, not the extraordinary, or the petty popularity, but the simple, pretty, and beautiful. It's much more basic than profound complexities we see around us.

What mental illness is like for me is having the light on in a room, and yet it is very dark in front of you. All around you, you can see and breathe and know that the world still does exist, but whenever you look ahead it is ALWAYS dark and heavy!

Schizophrenia is cruel, convicting, evil, again dark, lonely, frightening, and confusing. It is dark and heavy, putting obscure thoughts into your head. As many as four or five realities can go on at a time. You must figure out which one is real to function in the world around you. If you figure wrong, you get hospitalized, institutionalized, criticized, called a liar, and not believed by so-called professionals in crisis situations.

The walls talk and say strange things; nighttime is the worst. Electronics own you and dictate to your brain messages from those who have more authority than you have; you must listen or get in trouble. Oftentimes, they want you to harm yourself.

Your medications all call out at once: "Take me. If you take all of me, then these problems will never occur for you again, and you will be cured."

The Skeleton People show up, and their extremities (arms, feet, eyes, ears, and mouth) are on fire. They burn you horribly when they touch you and the burn goes away within minutes of them releasing you, but they don't let go without a fight. The Dark People haunt your mind and thoughts. They're painful to look at and make your heart and soul hurt and cry out desperately to God for help. Demons come and fight for your soul in front of you tooth and nail, clawing at you while they battle your Guardian Angel.

Sometimes it's just another person there talking to you, holding a conversation, yet no one else sees or hears this person you know is real and with whom you are having a conversation.

In your mental illness, you may even at times feel a raging wind in your gut that keeps telling you how much you have really let your family down since early childhood until now, much like a whirlwind of despair and torture. You have felt looping messages all your life. There is only one way to redeem yourself; that's to ask the King of Kings for His forgiveness and His grace, and maybe even cry a little to cleanse your soul.

Grandma Scheschi used to say, "It is said that the Holy Spirit collects each and every tear you will ever cry

-- -- -- -- -- ✺ -- -- -- -- --

and turns them into a beautiful garden at the entrance way of your mansion up in Heaven when you get there, and it is a gorgeous display of the love that He felt for you when you cried those tears." She said this whenever she was visiting from Green Bay and I was having a hard time just hanging onto any kind of will to live.

-- -- -- -- -- ✺ -- -- -- -- --

The Other Way Around

Sounds drift into sight
And sights drift into sound.
Tangible seems intangible
And the other way around.
What seems real in one moment
In the next is torn and thrown.
The unreal is real, and the real is unreal,
In my mind, as far as thought.
Silence is overbearing as depth
It is brought on by night.
A touch is non-convincing as no-one
Is standing there behind.
Silence enthralls me.
As other sounds seep their way through,
Seeking to destroy what's left of me
and to make their way to you.

-- -- -- -- -- ✧ -- -- -- -- --

The Haunting

The haunting has come around again!
And I in DISTANT VOICE,
Tried to call on my inner strength
To ease my soul and mind.

Thoughts are moving rapidly
And the voices right behind.
Chattering-jumbled up again
With no sense of what I hear outside.

The entanglement I find myself in
It is worrisome but also familiar.
Reality is lost and then
It is also profoundly present.

I find myself getting lost inside again
In what others call my make-believe...
But for me, it is genuine
More real than you and me,
And the factual is somewhere in between.

-- -- -- -- -- ❧ -- -- -- -- --

Ghoulish Howls...

The wind blows in ghoulish howls,
As do voices in my soul,
Unnerving and scolding,
Scattered in the pieces of my heart.
Frightened, I try to look for strength,
To fight for a sound mind.
Running from the things I see,
Haunting sights that shatter me.
Never knowing what's behind,
Shadows crossing just
Within my sight.

-- -- -- -- -- ✺ -- -- -- -- --

Hitler In My Head

How do I live life? …
With Hitler in my head? …
I feel I am responsible
For a hundred-million deaths.

How do I live life? …
Where I have no mind control?
Voices are all around me
Like demons in my soul.

How do I live life? …
With war raging on.
A whirlwind of nonsense,
And a tailwind of disgrace.

How do I live life? …
With this war raging on
Inside my head…
Racing thoughts, voices,
And much confusion
It is where I seem to be!

Upon A Dream

'The way I see my Dad'

The sounds of fury, rage!
Waters rushing forcefully
And thrust upon a lure
Of massive anger.
Pounding upon rocks,
And mounds of rocks,
On the horizon seen.
Seen only by the wanton eyes
Upon a person's dream.

-- -- -- -- -- ✌ -- -- -- -- --

It's Three O'clock

"It's three o'clock
And all is well,"
The night guardsman cries,
And at that moment
When he turned around,
He caught a bullet
Between the eyes.

It's three o'clock
And I am wide awake,
With a jolt of great surprise,
I am alive and well
With anguish spells
And have no war
To compromise.

The bullet that
The watchman took—
It could well have been my own!
For I now have been long
Enthroned upon the cast
Of several stones.

There are wars we fight
By day and by night,
In which no guns are utilized,
But there is still wounded, maimed,
And the greatness of pain,
Still causalities of war.

Feuds

How can I express
Just how I feel
When I have no idea
What feelings are real.

We fight like dogs,
And live like fools.
To some,
It is just a game.

The fights go on
For days at a time.
They linger in our heads,
Even after a few days of peace.

What can I do,
To end the feud-
That still rages
In my head?

What am I thinking?
What can I do?
I want so much for it to end,
I want NO more feuds!

-- -- -- -- -- ✆ -- -- -- -- --

Branded A Failure

When morning breaks,
And a new day dawns,
I wake again to carry on.
I kneel to pray.
May I do one task, right?
'Cause failure, like the sun,
Doth shine bright!
Failure lingers in patterns—
That lasts and then dies.
It tangles my insides,
It pulls and it tears.
Never forgotten, 'cause
Reminders are there!
Heaven forbid, should
I fail once again, 'cause
I know that the pattern
Is renewed not to end!
For forgiveness never comes
To those undeserved,
They are branded a FAILURE,
In a cycle that does not curve!

-- -- -- -- -- ✎ -- -- -- -- --

Scrambled Thoughts

I'm insecure about what I feel

And at times I don't know

What's truly real.

It's hard to express

What's on my mind

'Cause I don't know the questions

To the answers I find.

My life's not in shambles,

Though at times it does seem

Yet, I struggle to do right

And wonder if wrong is the key.

My thoughts are all jumbled

Deep in my mind

And I don't know if it is answers or

It is questions that I find.

The more I try to sort things out,

The more scrambled they seem to be.

The harder I attempt to do things right,

The more wrong those things seem.

And if by chance I don't try those things

Scaled by right or wrong,

My emotions are much stronger

And that much is harder to unfold.

-- -- -- -- -- ✥ -- -- -- -- --

I'm walking in giant circles,

In a maze of do's and don'ts

With a secret path that I must find

To sort out my scrambled thoughts.

-- -- -- -- -- ✑ -- -- -- -- --

Who Am I?

Who am I?
I do not know,
Just lost inside
An empty soul.

Where am I?
I do not care, --
For my mind wanders
From here to there.

My mind wanders
Incessantly, with no
Structure, pattern,
Or direction
To where it goes.

How am I?
It is a mystery too!
If I do not know,
Then, how can you?

-- -- -- -- -- ✥ -- -- -- -- --

Life Is Hell

Life is Hell, goes the saying,
But it is what I really believe inside.
Nothing is fair or pleasing, -
But everything adds to my jumbled-up mind.
What can I do to make life fair?
Or to give myself a waking shake?
One that would change my outlook on life,
To believe that even life's
Most modest problems I can take!

-- -- -- -- -- ❧ -- -- -- -- --

I Wish I Could Write

I wish I could write …
My feelings down honestly
The way I used to do.
But I have been
Out of touch with them,
And it seems
No words will do.
I am not exactly
Numb you know,
Nor do I want to be.
I just want my emotions
To run smoothly again
And their expressions
To be free.

-- -- -- -- -- ✆ -- -- -- -- --

Darkness and Light...

This book is about the journey I have taken from the darkness of mental illness into the Light of Jesus' Love for me, and my faith journey getting there. It would not be safe to say that this was a smooth journey for me, as I still struggle. *It's not for me to tell if I will struggle with mental illness for the rest of my life or not, it's just for me to realize that Jesus is in this battle over my mind with and alongside me; I lean on Him when the fight gets too hard now.* It's up to me to choose what I do with this struggle, and Jesus wants me to turn it over to Him. It is by His stripes that I know I am healed even if that healing comes in my eternal life with Him.

Depression equals darkness, a shadow that hangs over you like an eclipse hiding the sun. It does its best to keep God's Son, Jesus' Light from coming through. I've only just begun to live by faith, even though I accepted Jesus in 2014 and rededicated my life in 2017. I was baptized last year on Sunday, October 27th, 2019. But, it was Friday, January 24th, 2020, that I realized that the darkness sometimes comes out of nowhere and kicks me in the rear end. I let the words of someone who was looking in from the outside hit my heart, and for a few hours, I almost gave it permission to destroy me. If I had allowed it to kill me, it would have had a profound effect on those that love me, especially one person in my life. I turned to my faith that night hungering for a safe person to talk to, so I cried a lot and spoke to Jesus.

I let one person's words, not my friend's words, but the spoken words of some of her former co-workers send me into a tailspin that only Jesus could pull me through. They spoke the words. I guess they were trying to be helpful, but that's not how it resonated with me.

My point is this: darkness blocks the light, even the light of a friend's love that is there if you let it. Darkness tends to tell you that you are toxic and unworthy. It tells you to go down the rabbit hole like the one in *Alice in Wonderland*, where everything is skewed and distorted. It's a confusing place to be in.

Do not let anyone take your light from you; lean on the light of Jesus because that's all that really matters. Down that rabbit hole, where you really cannot trust your reality, darkness wants you to turn out the light from your life and life itself.

Darkness is lonely and disheartening, devastating, and blinding. Darkness can come from moving, having a good friend move, the death of a loved one, the words of another person, the seasonal effect of the winter, and abuse -- no matter how it is dished out. It comes from loneliness, negative self-talk, financial troubles, and any number of things I have not mentioned.

Sometimes God allows darkness to come into our life so that we will turn to Him and follow Jesus. We need to remember that Jesus has already WON the battle over the darkness, and His light is eternal. As the Bible says in Nehemiah 8: 10, that the joy of the Lord is your (our) strength. I am one to say that joy equals light!

Every day that we live in this fallen world, we need to understand that there are entities that try to wipe the joy out of us and to turn off the light so that we cannot find our way; we must not let them. Don't let anyone or anything take your light or your joy. Psalm 27: 1, says, "the Lord is my light and my salvation." It's the same for us now. We just need to turn to Him, and He will carry us through the darkness, so that we will not lose our way, if we let him carry us.

Job 38: 15, says that the light disturbs the darkness and stops the arm that is raised in violence. And in Proverbs 4: 18-19, it says that the way of the righteous is like the first gleam of dawn, which shines ever brighter until the full light of day. But the direction of the wicked is like total darkness, they have no idea what they are stumbling over.

If you find yourself struggling and the darkness seems to be strangling you, look to Proverbs 3: 5-6, "Trust in the Lord with all your heart; do not depend on your own understanding. Seek His will in all you do, and He will show you the way."

In other words, if you put your trust in the Lord and put your faith in Him, He will put a light unto your path to light the way for you. This light is the love of Jesus Christ. He lived His life as an example for us to go by. Yet, in our sin and blindness, He stretched out His arms as far as the east is from the west and said, "Father, forgive them for they know not what they do" and then He gave His life for us.

I ask of you to choose to be of the light and to dare to disturb the darkness. Choose the joy of the Lord, and

-- -- -- -- -- ✺ -- -- -- -- --

convey His light through love, kind words, and deeds. Say to the world, "I have no place in my heart for darkness." Dare to make this world a brighter place!

The next section of this journey leaves much of the darkness behind. It starts transitioning into the light, although I still had not accepted Jesus or reflected faith within myself. Looking back at these poems, I do see a significant difference between the times when I was totally lost inside the mental illness and the abuse, leading to the point where I start to heal.

My healing process has taken years and a stable support network around me. At first, I just relished the healing powers of nature, and I worshipped. I let whatever my conception of God or my Higher Power was to speak to me through nature's peacefulness as well as through her turbulence; through nature's flowers, animals, trees, waters, and the wind itself.

-- -- -- -- -- ❧ -- -- -- -- --

The River

The river is rain
Which floods the ground
One desperate rainy eve.

I could never hear
The call at hand.
'Cause the words
Are hard to perceive.
But thoughts are words
That comes to mind, --

Words only
I can hear.

How clever is
The weatherman
Who projects,
Both thought and fear.

More clever yet,
Is the pen in hand, that writes
The words that are so DEAR!

-- -- -- -- -- ❧ -- -- -- -- --

A Memorial To "Blackie" The Cat

A pile of wet leaves
Was to his delight,
He jumped right in
With all his might.

The flowerpot is
A perfect place to play
And jump right out
In a jack-in-a-box way.

The sea pilings
That makes up the porch
Were his jungle gym
Where he did tricks galore!

But the pile of leaves
Were to his delight,
He dove right on in
With all his might.

-- -- -- -- -- ❧ -- -- -- -- --

Sometimes

Sometimes I hurt
And I don't know why.
And sometimes I cry
In my bed.

Sometimes I reach out
For God to help me.
And it seems He
Helps others instead.

Sometimes when I'm asleep
I have nightmares.
And sometimes I wake up
Screaming in pain.

Sometimes I lie awake
Thinking at night.
And Lord knows what
Goes through my mind.

I feel as though
I have no way of expressing
The feelings I have.
And that scares me more
Then you know.

My Jesus has taken
All the hurt
That's deep down inside.
And has brought healing
To my screaming soul.

Nature Lies Awaiting

While nature lies awaiting,
The birds dance through the sky,
The horse stands there grazing.
Please, sing this lullaby.

The cats are out prowling,
Please, why should you cry?
A young bird is singing
Its newborn lullaby.

Spring is here, the time is near,
For children to sing and shout!
Their voices are all calling,
The bats and balls are out.

While nature lies awaiting,
For the spirit from above.
The newborn grass is lying
And Spring, well; here it comes!

-- -- -- -- -- ⚮ -- -- -- -- --

Jesus Christ Was Worth It

After a suicide attempt and right before another attempt, I had challenged God to a duel and if I won, I would take my life. If God won, and I feared this, I would reluctantly turn my life over to Jesus.

Well, obviously God won, and I am so very GRATEFUL that He did! I would never have known what real commitment is, or unconditional Love, or true honor, integrity, compassion, loyalty, and PEACE. His winning the challenge has brought such a POWERFUL and BRIGHT RADIANT LIGHT into my life, I really do not know any other way to explain it, but I can say it is not an earthly light or any manmade light.

Not only has this light come into my life, but a warmth that defies all warmth and came into the depths of my soul. I say this because I know that I was turning stone, dead cold inside the realms of my soul. If God would have wanted to stop with my blessings at the Light and the Warmth, surrendering to Jesus Christ was worth it. He was worth it even if I wouldn't have had the added benefit of having my sins washed away and being adopted into God's family, so that I may inherit my home one day in Heaven.

In my salvation, I became stable in my mental state for two years and I became complacent, comfortable, and started to once again try to depend on self. I turned from my faith and attempted suicide several more times until finally rededicating my life in May of 2017.

-- -- -- -- -- ✣ -- -- -- -- --

I was baptized in Believer's Baptism on Sunday, October 27, 2019. It was one of the most profound, significant, and happiest days of my life. That day not only meant a lot to me, but it also touched many who had been praying for me and supporting me through thick and thin.

I have not been hospitalized for mental health reasons since November of 2017, according to one of my caregivers. I'm taking her word on that, as I've lost track.

-- -- -- -- -- ✍ -- -- -- -- --

A Healthy Life

I have not written a poem in a while.
So tonight, I think I will try.
There are so many questions
For me to ask: like when, where, why, and who?
When can I realize what is right for me?
Where can I find happiness,
If not at home and tonight?
Why can't I live a healthy life; one
Without voices, visions, and strife?
Who will understand me when I hear,
And see things beyond reality?

Yesterday, I had just given my heart to Jesus.
So, I guess He is the One who will understand me.
My Home will one day be a peaceful place,
Where I will care to live.
And because of newfound faith,
I know that He will one day restore me to a healthy life.

-- -- -- -- -- ❧ -- -- -- -- --

Deep Within Me

There is anger deep within me
That festers in my soul.
It eats away at my insides,
And it takes the place of love.

It is a disease that overwhelms me,
A fierceness that boils my blood.

I clench my fists to bear it,
And I grit my teeth to cope.
In the end, it overtook me,
My bloodshot eyes swell with tears.

The last chance I have of gaining control
Of this anger inside of me
It is a deep breath and silence…
Until it is bottled deep inside of me.

My temples are still pounding,
My eyes are red with rage!
My heart is still hard and aching.
My fists clench and unclench,
So, to work away from this rage.

At last, I can control it,
To bottle the anger up inside.
I hope the lid stays on tight -
So, the anger will not eat away my mind.

-- -- -- -- -- ❧ -- -- -- -- --

This anger does not come often,
It takes a great deal to push me to the edge!
So, I take it out on paper,
By this, I can persuade it to end.

After the words are written down,
With the anger on paper put,
Before I go to bed at night,
I give it all to my Jesus
for Him to write it in His Book.

This poem was a symbol of my life in the beginning of my faith journey. It was a mixture and conglomeration of feelings. It took a friend saying that it makes her extremely sad when she reads it, for me to realize what I was actually going through during that time in my life. It really is a sad poem because of all the pain that I buried and that pain being the source of my PTSD. I buried the times I had been abused, had a gun put to my head and someone playing Russian roulette with my life. The pain of being raped and not letting my family know, because I knew that they would not support me in my recovery. It represents the tragedies I had gone through in life and my resilience to make it through, only at a great emotional cost. But these struggles have molded me into the Believer that I am today, and the struggle is getting easier because of the family that has adopted me into their lives.

In A Box

If my memories
Are in a box
Deep within my mind
And I can choose
Which ones can
Fill that box,
I would like to decorate
It with all my happy times.
Let the lid be of laughter
And the four sides be
Of peace and love.

47

-- -- -- -- -- ∽ -- -- -- -- --

Let the bottom
For once not be so serious
And let it be filled with jokes.
On the inside, we can
Hide the pain; still yet,
Keeping the knowledge
Of where it brought me,
And the person
That I have become.

-- -- -- -- -- ✍ -- -- -- -- --

I Dream Of …

I dream of being patient.
I dream of being kind.
I dream of being helpful,
And licensed to help the mind.

I dream of going to college,
Of walking across the stage.
And getting my bachelor's, Master's,
And Ph.D. at an awful later age.

I dream of having a successful career
And of owning my own home.
I dream of being married
And never being alone.

I dream that my special friends and I
Make years of happy memories too.
I dream of watching Cecily grow
And having other honorary grandchildren too…
I dream of all the happy times,
And put away the sad.
I dream that all those horrible memories
Retreat and don't come back.

I dream of sleeping through every night
Six hours or even up to eight
Then I dream I wake up rested
And ready to face the days.

-- -- -- -- -- ✿ -- -- -- -- --

I dream of the peace
That I felt in Charleston
The first time Melissa took me there.
I dream of how I found
My inner meaning of safety
In the four days while we were there.

I dream of many vacations
And trips away from Boone.
I dream of financial freedom
And a little cash to spend.
I dream of losing lots of weight
And buying new clothes to wear.
Of having a new wardrobe,
And of feeling special on the inside
For the weight that I have lost.

I dream of being able to drive again
And to travel from here to there.
Always on the road
When my time is free from cares.

I dream of driving down country roads and
Of traveling to make up for
Those years of no vacations
To speak of.
Of just leaving
Town to go on the road to just anywhere...
Maybe even just to drive around.

I dream of so many marvelous things …

-- -- -- -- -- ✾ -- -- -- -- --

The Fence

There is a world
Outside the fence,
Out there…
A world I have never seen.
The fence outside is limiting.
But it limits only me.
Fear has kept me in so long.
And fear is the fence.
Yet, I want to see that world outside,
I imagine it is limitless...

The fence may be limiting,
But I will not let it shut me in.
I will find my faith in Jesus,
As He will help me climb the fence.
I never realized how big the world
Outside it was!
It amazes me every single day,
I pray I do not let my trauma history
Again, let the fence get in the way.

-- -- -- -- -- ✿ -- -- -- -- --

Foolish Fears

Afraid of going to sleep at night
    Of the unknown dreams to face
    Of escaping the realms of reality
    Of ghosts, monsters, or Death—
        All that lingers in this place.

Afraid of waking in the morning
    Of facing possibilities of a new day
    Of mistakes bound to be made
    Of lashing out in anger or accepting
        Misdirected blame.

Afraid of being an influence on others
    Of misguiding a young life
    Of setting bad examples for impressionable
        Young tender lives.

Afraid of expressing thoughts or feelings
    Of relinquishing any trust
    Of those who are abusive
    Of those who will use to their advantage
        Knowledge of these thoughts.

Afraid of being the failure everyone expects of me
Of quitting in the middle of things
    Of falling into this trap again
        This time never to escape.

Afraid of fights and arguments
    Of letting my guard down
    Of lashing out with cruelty
    Of not thinking before I speak

-- -- -- -- -- 🙠 -- -- -- -- --

Of having my heart harden
    And filling with more and more hate.

Afraid of gaining credit where credit isn't due
    Of abusing any power bestowed upon me
    Of the negligence, I feel within.

Afraid of haunting voices
    Of echoes, possibly from within
    Of unidentified sights and sounds
        Not of reality.

Afraid of being emotional
    Of caring and
    Of LOVE
Of expressing these feelings to anyone,

Afraid of any unknowns out there
    Of finances, school and such
    Of establishing myself as a failure
        To those not already keen to that fact
    Of giving up the fight, I face daily
    Not to commit suicide and for my mental health
    Of calling it quits like so many times I almost did.

-- -- -- -- -- ❦ -- -- -- -- --

Lessons Learned

The other day, I learned a precious lesson: the meaning of it was driven home the next day in Trauma & Recovery Group.

The lesson: *that I <u>do</u> mean something to others and that I have a purpose in this world; to other people, my life has great value, meaning, use, purpose, and reverence.*

This is something that I must work on accepting about myself, and in T & R Group the other day, I knew I was not alone in this venture of self-acceptance. Why is it so hard for us women who have been abused since childhood or who have low self-esteem for any reason just easily incorporate this belief system into our lives?

The other day, Melissa left a bouquet of flowers on the handle of my screen door while I was cleaning the kitchen. She wanted to surprise me without me knowing it was her until the right moment. *"It meant more that way,"* *she said, "and sometimes the sweetest surprises with the best messages that come from the heart are unexpected and unannounced."* I did not get that until the group the day after. Our topic, "Actions speak louder than words" said it all. But the question wasn't only speaking of positive and negative actions towards others or toward our self, sometimes it is acting out for help.

Alcoholism, drug abuse, self-injurious behaviors, suicide attempts, eating disorders, smoking, cursing, and

54

out of character behavior that is getting out of hand, and other actions are examples. These actions do speak louder than words! They often leave caregivers and loved ones at a loss as to how best to help the one crying out for help.

Through group discussion and Melissa's gift of flowers, *I began to realize I have something to give to this world.* I've been getting hints of these lessons and clues to my life's purpose for some time now. It seems to be and feels like the right time to explore, continue, write about, and live-out my purpose in life right now. It is to be an author and a support person to my friends and family. My family being: my Mom, Melissa's family, Christina, Douglas, Audrey, Merrilee, Bonnie, Deneice, Wanda, and last, but not least, my church family especially my Sunday School Class. They are the key people in my life, my key supports. I would never even have attempted to get this book published without their support.

Douglas has encouraged me to keep writing and communicating with the outside world over a spread of several years. The Poem, "You and I" was written about Douglas and myself walking through our mental illness/schizophrenia together at a hard time during his life after he had supported me through so many difficult times in my life.

One of the best in-patient doctors that I have ever had, Dr. Musick, explained the schizophrenic brain to me by comparing it to eggs. The schizophrenic mind is like a scrambled egg, and most people walk around with a basically healthy functioning brain sunny-side up or over-

-- -- -- -- -- ✌ -- -- -- -- --

easy. When they have an off day or go through some difficulties the edges of their eggs may get a little scorched or distorted. Their yolks will dry-up if they hit an awful time in their lives, but their brains do not have chemical imbalances like those that a schizophrenic brain has

(distorted/scrambled), so they bounce back quicker. I am also bipolar, and I compare these seasons to a hard-boiled egg with its hills of extreme ups and extreme downs having smooth, slick edges; therefore, I may/can cycle rapidly.

In my darkest writing, you will experience depression in my book (depression equals the muck of an egg yolk in an over cooked over-easy egg), which conveys the lowest moments of my emotional upheaval, my experiences, and my imbalances. In writing the poems in the schizophrenia section of this poetry book, I was able to communicate with my mental health teams over the years. I had gone a significant period in my life locked inside myself, within what I call my scrambled egg mind. Without these writings, I would not have otherwise been able to communicate with the outside world.

-- -- -- -- -- ✃ -- -- -- -- --

One Step At A Time

One step at a time
That's all it takes,
It does not matter
If I make mistakes.

One day at a time,
Take it stride by stride.
Do not yield to tension,
But to peace of mind.

One step at a time,
That's all it takes.
Even by doing my best,
I will make mistakes.

Take one step backwards
If there is a need.
Life is not a race,
Do not set any speed.

One step at a time,
And if by chance I can't,
It really would not matter
If I were to just stand.

The next step is future,
The last step was past.
Take this step now,
To do the very best that I can!

-- -- -- -- -- ❦ -- -- -- -- --

Trust In The One

The darkness lingers.
The storm inside rages on.
The voices are unsilenced.
It'll be like this 'til dawn.

The fear is inside me,
Will I get sick again?
I don't like what's inside me:
The voices I hear.

I can only trust in the one,
Who carries me through!
He'll deliver me this time,
As He has the other times too.
I was not strong enough,
Therefore, I know that He had to
Carry me to get me through.

-- -- -- -- -- ❧ -- -- -- -- --

Freedom To Write

I like the freedom
That I have when I write,
And that I get to express
The thoughts and feelings I have.
A sheet of paper
Is non-judgmental,
Unlike the human ear.
Feelings do not get hurt,
Nor do arguments start.
Opinions written down
On a sheet of paper,
Can come from
Deep within
The human heart.

-- -- -- -- -- ᔥ -- -- -- -- --

A Warmth

I feel a warmth
In my heart,
That can only
Come from God.
I have a spring
In my steps,
That can only come
From Agape Love!

-- -- -- -- -- ❧ -- -- -- -- --

Spirit Battle

The power of the spirit world
Greater than my own,
The battle fought within
My body and my soul
It is long and heavy.
It takes compassion,
Feelings and love from my heart.
The battle is over life and death.
Over which will consume me.
The time is always now and
It is over my most significant needs.
My most significant needs are to be Heaven bound,
And to have Jesus in my heart.
I've just turned my life to Him recently,
And am confused as to when and where
My faith will start.

-- -- -- -- -- ✺ -- -- -- -- --

Turbulence!

My enemy is near!
I cannot see him here,
But I know that
He is in this room.
He surrounds me,
As if he were water
Engulfing every fiber
Of my existence…

I cannot fight him,
But I know
The One who can!
I rest in His assurance
That He will deliver
Me somehow!

I disappear
From my body,
And feel me burning
Down in Hell…
But I know that
That's not where I am going
Because of my Faith
In the Light of Christ!

-- -- -- -- -- ✺ -- -- -- -- --

I Feel So Lost

Lord: You know I feel so lost
And that I am looking for Your arms.
Lord, please help me find my way,
I want to worship You today.

Lord: You know I feel so lost
And I am searching in the dark
To find a pinpoint of Your light.
Lord, please guide me to Your side.

Lord: You know I feel so lost
And I am looking for my way.
Lord, I know You guard and guide,
Please lead me to Your side today.

Lord: you know I feel so lost
For I have sinned, and I have strayed.
Yet Lord; You've always led me home,
And once I found my way in You,
You forgave me of my sins.

-- -- -- -- -- ✥ -- -- -- -- --

Connection To The Cross

I know that for my sin,
Jesus came down to earth to die
By giving His life on the infamous cross.
Before I asked him into my life,
My heart and my soul were lost,
But now that I know Him,
I live inside His love and sacrifice.
My soul knows the Salvation
He really gave me
Because I believe in Him.
As I sacrificed my heart and life for Him,
By walking within the light of the cross,
I feel the redemption that Jesus gives.
He gives graciously to those who believe
Through His powerful love
By making the connection to the cross.

-- -- -- -- -- ❧ -- -- -- -- --

I Am Thankful

In all things I am thankful,
Is what the Lord teaches me!
But there is one thing I question,
And that is not a right-left up to me.

There is one thing I have expected,
No matter the time or the day.
Is that not all of life's follies,
Dare to go my way.

I have conquered many leaps and bounds.
I have won my share of games!
The question I have stored
In my mind remains.

It is not a question of morals,
Or have I greatly sinned?
It is not a question I deserve to ask
Or to have the answer sent.

It is not a question of colors,
Not black or white.
But it defeats most boundaries and cornerstones
Laid down in people's lives.

It is a question I must handle
And one that I must fight.
For the answer may not come easy,
But then again, it might.

Therefore, in all things I am thankful,
Whether they be good or bad.
This is the way I must live my life:
To obey my God's commands.

Your Glory, Lord

My eyes have seen Your glory, Lord
Coming down to visit me.
You are telling me that
I deserve Your Love,
And to rest inside sanity.
You are teaching me to face my fears,
Having you along my side,
Holding my hand
Ever so tightly Lord:
You will not let Your grip
Release my hand,
Because You squeezed it tight.
You have me give my fears to You,
And as I am faithful in my
Belief and in my prayers,
All my hopes and dreams
Will come true, Lord,
As I place my faith in You

-- -- -- -- -- ⋖ -- -- -- -- --

Rush Hour
view from my hospital window

Room 919
Cancer Care Unit
Baptist Hospital, Winston-Salem

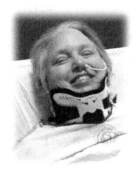

I _do_ NOT have cancer! I was in the cancer center for another issue.

As I sit here in my hospital room, I look out the window to see rush-hour traffic on NC I-40 in Winston-Salem. I wonder where that traffic is traveling: in one direction to the beach, the mountains in the other.

The traffic -- continually starting stopping, weaving in and out, never-ending at this time of the day. I realize that it is this time of the day in my life, my health situation also stumbling, starting, moving, and pressing

forward. But there are obstacles in the way, as well.

The traffic jam of life: will I choose to endure or just park and wait, waiting through uncertainty?

I have never waited before, but I am tired, tired of the constant uphill battle, tired of feeling sick, tired of the surgeries, tired of fighting. What else do I have but the fight; what would Missy

68

-- -- -- -- -- ❧ -- -- -- -- --

Hydi-Ann do if I stopped fighting? What would this honestly say about my faith? Question upon question, and the only answer seems to come from the rush hour traffic: it moves slowly at times, steadily at other times. Still pressing forward engaged in a purpose, always going ahead.

I only need to decide which direction I should turn my life. I do not have to decide this right now. Now, the decision needs to be: will I press forward, move ahead, weave in and out until I finally make my destination, and finally make it home?

Of course, I do not want to be sick anymore, especially as unhealthy as I have been.

I want my health back, and I want to enjoy Missy Hydi-Ann every single day of the week, month, and year. Year in and year out the two of us, both of whom have lost, but in our loss, we found each other, and that, my friend, is worth the fight.

I just need a few hours break to rest and regain my strength and then:

I will play cards again.

I will fight…!

-- -- -- -- -- ❦ -- -- -- -- --

"You and I" is about Douglas and me and our friendship, as well as support of one another. We suffer in the grip of mental illness and paranoid schizophrenia, or schizoaffective disorder. He has been blessed to be more stable than I have been over the years, but when I wrote this poem, he was having a difficult time of it.

I have been blessed to have known Douglas, and I consider him to be like my younger and much TALLER brother. We currently live across the state from each other, but we stay in good contact.

Remember Douglas, if ever you need a hug, put your right arm across your left shoulder and your left arm across your right shoulder, then squeeze, and that's a HUG from me!

You And I

We will overcome,
The two of us, you and I!
For we have suffered
In front of the naked guns,
Underneath the butcher's eye!

We will overcome,
The two of us you and I!
One step here, and a Hand-Up there:
But, across the way,
We will make it today.

-- -- -- -- -- ❧ -- -- -- -- --

We will overcome,
The two of us, you and I!
Faith and a Prayer.
Jesus, are you out there?
He will answer us and our needs tonight!

We will overcome,
The two of us, you and I!
Being Awake and Aware,
Knowing from before!
Yes, the Lord is there, and He Does Care!

-- -- -- -- -- ∾ -- -- -- -- --

This poem was written during my first Easter
as a Christian Believer.
It expresses the overwhelming joy I felt
that first Easter celebration.

We Sing

We sing in times of pleasure,
That our hearts remain happy and gay.
We sing in times of peace,
That our hearts know calmness.
We sing in times of celebration,
That our hearts can rejoice.
We sing when we worship,
That our hearts can praise the Lord.

-- -- -- -- -- ✑ -- -- -- -- --

But A Lifetime

Jesus, come by the mountain
Or the river beside.
Love lasts forever,
That cannot be denied,

Praises last a lifetime,
While beauty fills the air.
Lord, come to this fountain
And I will show I really care.

Peaceful scenes are but a moment,
And war will last a year.
Lord, how can I tell you,
It is not death that I fear.

I have cried just one raindrop
From the bottom of my heart.
Can that moment be forgotten,
And that year from Love depart?

I have not but a lifetime
To do Your will for me,
To do as You would have me do
And to spread Your Love and Peace.

Love lasts forever!
Let's all show we really care!
Giving Him our hearts and praise,
To make Peace the promise
That we will let it fill the air.

73

-- -- -- -- -- ✑ -- -- -- -- --

Between Me, Myself, and I ...

I thought I had an understanding
At this point.
About the confidence,
I would hold deep down inside.
I wouldn't let a single soul discourage me.
Least, not one as toxic as he.
I would put on the shield of God,
And the darts would fall-
Down upon his angry him.
I would not let his discouraging words
Deepen my doubts about going to school,
Instead, I'd hang onto the confidence I had.
No longer broken into smithereens,
The hard work I've done to bend
Some of the crooked rules I've faced
To go back to school that
I've lessened yet again!
I listened to him again
Saying: "you, dumb fool
You are too stupid to go to school."
Just today, I rekindled a spark
And a strong relationship between
Me, myself, and I.
I had an intense conversation
Between me, myself, and I.
I told Me not to let anyone else's doubts
Come between your dreams and you!
Not to let them make those dreams die,
You can do anything at all in life if
You lead with Christ and prayers, and truth.

-- -- -- -- -- ❧ -- -- -- -- --

If

If I could have
One wish of mine,
One dream, I would know
To come true,
I would wish for peace in mind
'Cause I know that
I cannot please you.
If I could do just one thing right,
Whether it be great or small.
Would you be willing to acknowledge it?
Or would it ever happen
At all?

-- -- -- -- -- ❧ -- -- -- -- --

Central Love

When you are all alone
And you feel despair,
There is someone there
Who really cares.

When you start to wonder,
What shall I do?
The answer will
Surely come to you.

There's a central love
And it's all around,
It's spreading the gospel
From town to town.

When you are feeling down,
Do not despair,
The central love
Is everywhere!

-- -- -- -- -- ✍ -- -- -- -- --

What I See

No one sees what I see,
There is beauty all around!
People look to war and hate,
While I look to God and love.

The beauty of a mountainside,
And the valley down below.
To them, it's another hill to climb,
Another fall to undergo.

Rain makes the air cleaner
And the grass greener.
They relate rain to their hurt inside,
And all the tears that they have cried.

I see the sun rising in the dawn
And setting again at dusk.
People see a day as a lifetime,
And night as everlasting rest.

No one sees what I see,
There is beauty all around!
People look to war and hate,
While I look to God and love.

-- -- -- -- -- ❧ -- -- -- -- --

Faith

Faith believes in
Never-ending ties.
On songs with words
Of lullabies.

God gave us faith
To hope and share
The love of Christ
Which is pure and rare.

Faith is a gift
Which all men have.
The love of God,
And the gift of a man.

Faith is to soar
Above the sky,
Like an eagle flying
To pass us by.

Faith is believing
In love and life.
It believes in God,
Who rules on high!

Faith is the love
Which is shared by Christ:
Who came down to earth
And laid down his life!

-- -- -- -- -- ❧ -- -- -- -- --

Think Of Life

To think of life,
I only knew,
To think one thought,
It is trite and true.

To take a breath
And to take it now,
Gives the life
Therefore, it gives the thought.

To touch the earth
Is soil moist and brown.
This bringing to my mind,
the beauty
Of both trees and flowers.

To think of water,
Moist and wet,
Gives life to all
Flower, beast, and men.

To think of life,
I only knew,
To think one thought
It is trite and true!

-- -- -- -- -- ◦§ -- -- -- -- --

To The Cross On My Knees

When I first saw the light
Of my salvation, I was lost
As a sinner could be.
I was a liar and a cheater,
There was no hope for me.
But, because of the prayers
Of those who loved me,
I came to the Cross on my knees.
Before I knew it, the turmoil in my soul,
Suddenly melted into peace.
Yes, there are still days, where I fall short,
Moments when it seems my faith
Has all but failed.
But it is in these moments that I turn to God,
I know that I am carried by the Lord Himself.

-- -- -- -- -- ✺ -- -- -- -- --

Please, Dear Mr. Jesus

Please, Dear Mr. Jesus,
I really need to talk to you.
I'm so messed up inside
That I don't know what to do
There is so much that I hear
Outside my head
That I don't understand.
Two weeks in the new memories
Didn't make it easier to take.
I wonder if the torment
Is here forever now to stay?
Please, Mr. Jesus,
Help me through this life
Because left to my own devices
I know I would not survive.
Give me strength, Mr. Jesus, Please,
I've come this far
Because of you.
I know that Mr. Jesus,
You won't let
Me down right now, as I am
Holding to your promises
Between me, God, and You.
Thank you, Mr. Jesus,
For lending me your ear.
Thank you for helping me
Through these times and tears. Amen

-- -- -- -- -- ✌ -- -- -- -- --

The Bird's Song

There was a cool breeze,
Not a sound, except
The sound of rustling leaves,
And of the bird's song.
Not a bad sound at all.
It was a peaceful, quiet,
Nonviolent, and yet
Charming sound.
There was a flock of birds
Overhead flying east
With the clouds.
Just gliding along
Moving peacefully
Through the blue sky.
There was a Robin
In the pecan tree
Behind me, chirping away.
A horse was grazing
In the field
To the left of me.
A black cat
Prowled skillfully
Through the tall grass
In the field.
Another horse was
Galloping through the field,
As a rabbit dashed out of its
Hiding place into the woods
Nearby.

-- -- -- -- -- ✍ -- -- -- -- --

But the most impressing,
And charming of these events,
Was the peaceful sound
Of the bird's song.

-- -- -- -- -- ❧ -- -- -- -- --

Family

Family is a complicated thing to try to define or to explain. On some household decorations, one may read a saying that goes like this: "Family, where life begins, and Love never ends." I will not argue with that saying if I have the right to change it to: "Family, where True Life begins, and Love will never end." Because that is how it has happened in my life with Melissa's family, and I have been very blessed by it.

Our story began when Melissa approached me while I was in crisis in the ER at the medical center. She is a nurse supervisor for the ER and was on duty that day, during one of the most desperate and vulnerable times of my life. I did not know it then, but looking back at it, it was in her life too. I had just stabbed myself the night before thinking I was fighting off what was a hallucination and thought it was the hallucination that had stuck me. I spent the night fighting the nurses, doctor, and security staff as well as a couple of sheriff's deputies. The more they medicated me and held me down the more I fought, and I was convinced that they were not human beings that I was fighting. Melissa knew that if they were to treat me that they would have to get me to stop fighting and so she approached me calmly, and we talked. She treated me like I was a human being and not a wild animal or freak of nature.

I related to her, and I needed to trust someone, she convinced me that she was my friend. Little did I know it, but that day she approached me was her first day back at

84

work after a tragedy had occurred in her life. We have been friends ever since. There has always been a sisterhood-like connection, between the two of us; I guess, at least I felt it, that feeling still encompasses me today.

I met Bobby, Melissa's oldest son, first. Melissa and Bobby came over to take me out to eat after I got out of the hospital. I later realized that when I met Bobby and the reception, I had gotten from him; it was the second indication (Melissa being the first) of how I was already a part of their family. Kimberly's baby shower was just the thread that finished the garment. It was the next time that I would meet family members, her other son Mathew, and daughters Kambrey and Kimberly, and her parents and stepparents.

You see, it did not matter to Melissa's family how much my family hated me, or rejected me, or even that I had schizophrenia, PTSD, or self-injurious behaviors. What mattered to them was that I was a person who needed to be needed and that Melissa loved me and accepted me. They knew that I had a lot to give back. The whole Gragg family saw this empty shell of a person and gave this person a filling.

Together we have celebrated Cecily's birth, three Christmas days, Valentines, Easters, and birthdays. We've had game nights together. I am an Honorary Grandmother to Cecily (and loving it) and will be to all future Gragg children.

My love for Melissa's family and their love for me gave me the will to live. I haven't overdosed, cut, or stabbed myself in a long time now. I am working on my problems with eating with love I feel from them, even when they don't approve of my actions. Well, let's just say that I will conquer that too.

Family, where True Life begins, and LOVE NEVER ends...

Let me explain why I say: "true life begins." There is no real life if one is so unhappy that every day, all one can think about is ways to die. When a friend steps in from nowhere and suddenly makes you a part of their family as if you belonged a lifetime ago, that is special and "TRUE LIFE" does and has begun because you know that you belong. You are an integral piece of a whole and you fit in the puzzle for a change. You are no longer a square piece trying to fit in a round hole.

With a family behind you, speaking for myself anyway, I find a power inside that was never there before. A special kind of strength that is empowering. It is this force, strength, and love that helps me to grow as a person. I want to improve myself every day and be better spiritually, mentally, and physically for them and because of them.

I want to be there to see my honorary grandchildren grow. I want to be present as my new family goes through changes: like marriages, childbirths, grandchildren, and God-willing great-grandchildren. I want to experience vacations with them, birthdays, game nights, holidays, and whatever experiences or memories we will have together. "Yes, indeed, True Life has begun."

-- -- -- -- -- ✖ -- -- -- -- --

Badge of Honor

C.S. Lewis said, *"True Friends don't spend time gazing into each other's eyes. They show great tenderness toward each other, but they face in the same direction, toward common projects, interests, goals, and above all, toward a common Lord."*

As I consider the many blessings that God has given to me, I remember to thank Him, most of all, for my many friends! He has chosen to place many people in my life's path. People who have both touched my life and whose lives I feel my life has reached, knowing that I Have Been Richly Blessed by my friends and their presence in my life.

I do not know how my life would have turned out without Bobby Flores, Ruth Batchelor, Yvonne, Kyle, Douglas, Christina, Melissa, Deneice, and Wanda, or Audrey, Bonnie, Merrilee, and so many others. I do know that it would have been so empty and more difficult. Perhaps even, I would not have made it without one of them by my side. I do know that God answered my prayers in the nick of time when He then sent each one of them into my life!

I am richly blessed by my friends! I live every day knowing that I am loved in the way they love me or in a similar manner in which I LOVE them. It feels good to me knowing that I mean so much to many different people and that I touched their lives like they touched mine. I can only hope that my friends feel as blessed by my friendship as I do theirs. I even have a couple of new

-- -- -- -- -- ✍ -- -- -- -- --

friends whose friendship means so very much to me: Lisa, my neighbor, and Ginger and her Golden Retriever,-Elsa.

Friendship: defined by Merriam Webster's Collegiate Dictionary as the quality or state of being friendly. Friendly is defined as showing kindness or goodwill, cheerful, comforting. A friend is one who is not hostile. Another dictionary says that a friend is a favored companion, a person who is attached to another by feelings of affection.

To me, a friend and friendship is so much more: it's honor, loyalty, honesty, trust, trustworthiness, compassion, joyfulness. It includes humor, tears, trials, growth, and triumphs. It encompasses courage that surrounds the other's fears; it wipes out ever walking alone again because, with good friends by your side, this just does not have to happen ever again. It means family-by-proxy when your birth family is absent or doesn't give a damn. It means being loved and having someone to LOVE!

C.S. Lewis was right, friends show great tenderness towards each other, only they face in the same direction with common goals, plans, projects, interests, and above all, toward a common Lord. But, added to this is a devoted Love for each other.

I hold it so dear to my heart that my friends all follow in Jesus' footsteps. It helps me in my faith and walk. I couldn't hold on without witnessing the kind of faith that they have shown me in their hard times. I am glad that they trust my faith enough to come to me to talk through their troubles. To ask for someone just to listen to them without saying a word, or even someone trusted enough to give simple advice or just to pray for them. It seems that even when I feel weak in my own life, I can be strong, stable, and healthy for my friends, and what they are going through in their lives. This feels good to me, and important or essential somehow because it makes me stronger than I think I am.

Let's go back to friendship and what it means. Friendship; priceless and timeless, expands beyond space, beyond death, beyond distance, and time. It's endless, and it is a bond that one must never take for granted; because it is a beautiful gift of trust and of selflessness that another has bestowed upon you. Friendship is a badge of honor; one must wear it with honor. It is rich, and if one has just a single friend that is loyal, true, and trustworthy, then one is wealthy indeed.

Dear Lord,

Thank you so very much, Father, for sending me all my wonderful FRIENDS that you have thoughtfully touched my life with. Let our friendships Honor You, Lord, as we walk through this life together following the footsteps of Your Son, Jesus. May we grow stronger in our Faith together, holding each other up and giving momentum and strength to one another; so that we may hold steadfast to Your Promises, Your Presence, and Your Word. Thank You, Father, for putting us in each other's lives to walk this life together and in support of one another, to help teach each other about faith and lead each other to You.   Amen

July 4, 2019

-- -- -- -- -- ✍ -- -- -- -- --

Melissa Ford Gragg RN, WMC-ER
You Are the Nurse I Call Friend!

You weren't just another nurse
Trying to make the crossing easier.
You were a special nurse
Who wanted to make the crossing:
Wider, deeper, and more meaningful.
You took on a friendship
With a troubled soul,
And made the soul
More at rest and comforted,
All the while teaching me
What family really means.
It's making the passing
Wider, deeper, and more meaningful.

You aren't just another nurse
Who tried to make the crossing easier!
You are the special nurse,
Who took time to teach me, -
How to listen more intently,
With more care, empathy, and compassion.
You taught me to listen with my eyes
As well as my ears.
You taught me to speak lovingly
Without saying a word.
You were that special nurse
Who made my life, -
Wider, deeper, and more meaningful.

Julie C. Weidner

-- -- -- -- -- ❧ -- -- -- -- --

You Are Not Just Another Nurse!
You're the Nurse who turned my life around.
Making it wider, deeper,
And much more meaningful.
You are the nurse I call FRIEND!

-- -- -- -- -- ✿ -- -- -- -- --

What Does Safety Mean to Me?

If I had been asked this question several months ago, my answer would have been shaded differently from what it is now!

Then I would have had to say that safety was only in the company of my friends: Melissa, Christina, Kyle, Rebekah, Deneice, and at Mount Vernon Baptist Church. I would have NEEDED to have contemporary Christian music playing in my apartment all the time. I would have had to have the voices not to be fighting with each other consistently or to see skeleton people on fire frequently. My most straightforward answer to feeling safe would had to have been to have Hydi-Ann tell me that it is safe as she guarded us by her demeanor; without her, I am lost.

Afterward, I went for a period with excellent stability. I hadn't heard voices or seen scary things, and my answer changed to just keeping my good friends mentioned above near me. Hanging-out with them as much as possible and staying busy all the time. I was in school, so I would study almost continuously.: twenty-four hours a day if I could stay awake. I worked hard and had the highest grade in the class, and that felt safe. Until the pressure was on, but then the seizure came on February 7th. I had a head injury from it and couldn't continue in school because I could not look at a computer screen without significant headaches and nausea. My life, was NOT SAFE ANY LONGER! I went through a period of confusion and disappointment in myself.

Melissa and I went to Charleston on vacation from March 8th to March 12th. My whole view of what safety is to me changed on that vacation. I gained a new perspective that Melissa had tried so hard to teach me before. When we entered her condo and the peace I felt so suddenly there, I finally GOT IT!

Safety is more complicated than just not hallucinating, as in hearing and seeing things. It's more complicated than keeping busy, so you don't have time to pay attention to your delusions.

Yes, safety is being around your good friends, but it is so much more than that.

It's living with a sense that life is in front of you, and that the definition of life is ADVENTURE.

It's being able to say I'm glad I'm here! And that I'm All In! It's being not afraid to take risks if the risks get you to your dreams.

Safety is about peace and tranquility, living in a space that's worry-free and comfortable — having a place to call home and having a family to love and to come back to. Even if that family is a family that you have adopted into your life.

Safety is about friendship, a friendship that goes beyond measure, a bond that you know will never die. Safety goes deep, and safety goes beyond!

Safety is intense, safety is peaceful; safety is tranquil; safety is quiet, safety is all this! And safety is so much more!

-- -- -- -- -- ✑ -- -- -- -- --

Safety goes beyond what I can describe! I'm just glad I got to learn what it is in only four days: four of the most peaceful days of my life.

I learned that the different roads we travel on bring us to various destinations, some are rotten, and some are beautiful, and some are downright AWESOME!

Safety is finding the roads to beautiful and impressive destinations, and that gets you to the goals of your deepest dreams. So, Dream BIG!

-- -- -- -- -- &ogra; -- -- -- -- --

Hydi and the Chipmunks

It has been interesting since I have come home. We have knocked the pots and pans out of the cupboards at 2:00 am, and close to 3:00 am, twice! My neighbor said that she knew that I was home because she could hear Miss Hydi playing at night once again. We are still doing dishes before and after we eat. The before is because Hydi thinks that the cupboard is an excellent place to hide (or as we shall say Hyde!), and the plates make a lovely bed. Believe me, she thinks they are comfortable too! The bowls are a beautiful place to cuddle as well!

As far as diet goes, we have a constant run on the chipmunk diet: chipmunk stew, casserole, and soup, leftovers enough to feed the whole town of Boone.

Live chipmunk chases have taken place in the apartment daily for the past three days in a row. So far, every chipmunk that was inside, I do believe, has been accounted for. If we missed any, I shall let you know of the stench or of the births. However they may occur!

The count so far is 27 dead and eaten? (Not really!) Two Robins in mid-flight, baked, and roasted? (Not really!) and three, make it four, chased -- one going on this moment. You will have to excuse me as I am about to chase a cat and then a chipmunk! (FOR REAL!)

95

-- -- -- -- -- ✺ -- -- -- -- --

Falling Short
"A Love Letter to my Cat, Hydi-Ann"

Hydi,
I want you to know
That my love for you is never-ending!
I know that I fall short when it comes to
Waking up in the morning
To feed you on time,
But you will never go hungry
As you had before I rescued you!

I fall short when it comes to
Playing with you at ALL Hours of the night
As we used to play
Before I learned how to sleep
At night once again.

I fall short at giving you "attentions"
When I am working on a writing project
Or on computer-study activities.
I know you are used to me
Stopping whatever I am doing
Just for you.

I do want you to know; however,
That I will Never Ever fall short
In the areas that
Falling short is inexcusable!

-- -- -- -- -- ✍ -- -- -- -- --

I will always Love you
With a Never-ending LOVE!
I will always give you "attentions"
Every day that I am home with you.

I will always find you
Veterinary care as you may require it
For whatever reason.

I will always from the day I adopted you,
Keep you from harm
To the best of my abilities
As sometimes you do escape
And I am powerless then.

I will always protect you from abuse
Like you had suffered before I rescued you.
Like I said to you
Every single day that
You have been in my life:
"You are magical, wonderful,
Whimsical, imaginative,
And I will Always Love you!
Hydi-Ann Marie, when it counts,
I will Never fall short.

-- -- -- -- -- ✥ -- -- -- -- --

Moment Made Of Gold

I have squandered my existence
For a moment made of gold,
Where there are no voices,
Shadows or things that are not real.
I am not so sure of what I have done.
I have given Jesus my life to have.
This moment seems like a costly one,
And I do not know how
I will pay it off.

I only pray that
The golden moment comes soon,
For my spirit can take no more.
I also hope that it will last,
As I have just now this moment met the Lord.
I hate the illusions, the things that aren't real,
Can He really carry them away?
I ask this because I see these things every single day.

My Savior, Jesus said,
"Jewel, come to Me; you need not be afraid.
You no longer need to live in this pain."

-- -- -- -- -- ✍ -- -- -- -- --

The Touch

The darkness is overbearing,
As the depth is brought on by night!
A touch is non-convincing,
There's no one standing there behind.
The halls are filled with snoring,
As other sounds vanish in thin air.
The world seems dead
And idle:

There is no hypocrisy
To be observed
In the dark night atmosphere.

Silence enthralls itself
Upon me,
Few sounds sift
Their way through.

The only sounds of pencil scratches
As it rubs across the page,
Cricket chirps are muttered
And seep through the window, pain-

When the glass is shut,
The sound is gone.
I am alone once again.

The lonely hours
Are the dark ones.

-- -- -- -- -- ❧ -- -- -- -- --

Yes, the lonely hours
Are the dark ones,
But Jesus is by my side!
That touch is his hand on my shoulder
Giving me an eagerness to write.

My pencil cannot write fast enough
To record my fleeting thoughts,
But at least it is not
The voices this time
That control my mind right now!

-- -- -- -- -- ✎ -- -- -- -- --

The Awakening

As the wind blows
Through the treetops,
And the leaves begin to fall,
It's the spirit of winter
And the spirit conquers all.
It's like a rest
For the flower
Until the spirit
Has come and gone.
It's a peaceful moment
In the making.
But will the peace linger on?
With the spring comes the awakening,
The renewal of life.
It is like the resurrection
Of the human sacrifice!

-- -- -- -- -- ✆ -- -- -- -- --

Jesus, To the Ends Of the World

Jesus loves me...
Yes, He loves me, so...
So, I will follow...

Jesus guides me...
Where he leads me...
I don't know...
But I will follow!
Yes, I will follow Him...
To the ends of the world.

Jesus loves me...
Yes, He loves me, so...
So, I will follow...

He forgives me!
Won't you forgive me?
Can't I forgive me?
He has guided me ...
Forgiveness is inside of me.
Wow! The power of His guidance
And of His love.
His grace is freely given...
Yes, given to all of us today.

Jesus loves me...
Yes, He loves me so!
So, I will follow...
Yes, I will follow Him!
To the ends of the world.

-- -- -- -- -- ❧ -- -- -- -- --

Across The Room

If God were sitting
In a chair across
The room from me,
What kind of questions
Would I ask Him
If that were a right for me?

I would ask why
The colors of the rainbow?
R-O-Y-G-B-I-V
And, the order that they come in.

I would ask why
Do only birds have wings?
And, what would it feel like
To fly like them?

I would ask to live
Under a waterfall.
So it's beauty I can
Always see.

I would ask what it would be like
To be as tall as the tallest tree.
How much would the perspective
Of life change for me?

-- -- -- -- -- ❧ -- -- -- -- --

I Am …

I have embraced the earth
Since the beginning of time
With my melodies and rhymes.

I can move in calmness and in peace
Persuading babies into sleep.

I can rush hurriedly
With extreme excitement.
But I am never early or late.

I can express joy, love, and happiness.
I can show hurt, anger, or pain.

I can cause people to
Laugh, cry, or reason.
I can describe
Weather, days, and seasons.

I am older than a thousand
Or even a million years past.
Interpretations of me changes
With each new moment that passes.
I am as old as old can be.
But, with each new measure,
I become young again new and free.

-- -- -- -- -- ✧ -- -- -- -- --

Time cannot stop me from going on
And touching the hearts and souls
Of every living creature.
I am the oldest thing created.
Yet, every day, I am also the youngest.

I can describe any
Thought, emotion, and feeling.
Or, even God, nature, and any human.

I am NEVER the SAME
From one moment to the next.
Like all things, I CHANGE.

I may be very simple or very complex.
I may be soft and slow or harsh and fast.
Or any range between.

You may HEAR me in the bird's SONG,
On the radio, and on T.V.,
In the wind, you may hear a TUNE,
And in that TUNE is me…
I am written in measures
And counted in beats.
I have HARMONY and MELODY.
I can be played, hummed, and sung.

I can be a babbling brook, rustling leaves,
The wind against the tall reeds.
I AM . . .
  -- If you have not guessed already --   *Music!*

-- -- -- -- -- ✤ -- -- -- -- --

This Is Light and Grace
"Stone Cold"

The truth for me started to be lived out in my life on August 7, 2014. I was forty-seven years old and very lost. On this day, **I found a light that rushed into my life.** It was the first time since being a toddler that I had an actual deep desire to live. **I knew that I knew what true Love and Joy were. For the first time in my life that I can remember, I was content.**

The whole week before, a coldness had come over my body, spirit, and soul. Not a cold like one I can describe, it was worse than frostbite cold, bone-cold, or even stone cold. A coldness went beyond my body and spirit down into the deepest depths of my soul. No matter how hot the temperature would get, I was still freezing, only worse, and did not know why. My soul was turning DEAD COLD: my soul was dying, the candle was going out, and there was no time left for me if I did not turn to Jesus. I was not only freezing on the outside, but on the inside as well; to a depth that I can still grievously remember, but cannot even begin to understand or to describe. I knew that I was alive, but not living, and living, but not alive in some colossal way. I was not really living, and I just did not know why. I was not dead quite yet, either.

On August 7th, 2014, I talked to Mary. She was my ACT-Team therapist. She spoke to me about Jesus and God. She lovingly and genuinely laid it all out, plain and simple. I only half-heartedly listened to the "Jesus Junk," (or so I thought what it was at the time). After she left, I overdosed on sleeping pills, Xanax, and my heart medicine as I challenged God.

Little did I know that Mary was praying for me, and God would take me on and accept my challenge. Well, God, He answered the charge I handed to Him, and that really ticked me off because I had a huge death wish and had fully intended to go through with killing myself that night. Because God won the challenge and because I still prided myself as an "honest and honorable person," I honored my end of the deal in case this "Jesus person and God Creator" was real. Therefore, I accepted Jesus into my heart. In addition, as a result, a light so amazing shined from a desperate darkness that was within; it even lit up the midnight sky.

Along with the light, came a gentle warmth that blanketed me with an unconditional Love and Acceptance. I belong to Him through Redemption (Gal. 4: 4-5) and by His Devotion (Heb. 13: 5, John 1: 12-13, Phil. 3: 20). Therefore, I was being marked by adoption as His daughter (Gal. 4:4-5, Hebrews 13:5, John 1:12-13) and given citizenship in His Kingdom in Heaven (Phil. 3:20, Phil. 4:1-3). To be totally honest with you, I did not know what I was getting myself into. Now I am GRATEFUL that I am here. That blanketing, loving, gentle warmth chased the dead, stone cold away from my spirit and soul, and it still comforts me to this day. That is why I am writing this testimony of Peace and Faith (Romans 5: 1-2)

I cannot describe the feeling of how POWERFUL, Complete, Un-conditional, Gentle, and Genuine this

-- -- -- -- -- ❧ -- -- -- -- --

warmth of LOVE felt and still feels. I only can tell you that you can have it too, if you want it. It is a feeling that I never want to forget or be without.

-- -- -- -- -- ⁊ -- -- -- -- --

Fleeing From the Light

In writing Stone Cold, I told the story leading up to what I now consider the most beautiful day of my life, but I would not have called it that back then.

It was a difficult, frightening, almost terrifying time for me, and so much of my life was about to change, even if the change would be both instantaneous in one aspect and gradual enough to take years in another. For me to think that Jesus is Lord and that there is a Father-God, and a Holy Spirit and that they exist as the Three in One, yet separate of themselves, playing different roles in the deity. My mind could not understand it. I ran from it and I feared it.

After all, I had really screwed up my life in a significant kind of way: I had tried to destroy this temple (my body and soul), I was a liar, and I was a coward. I surely did not want to face an omnipotent Being/Lord/God with these sins under my belt. I had already talked myself into believing I was the only person on the face of the earth who did not deserve forgiveness; the messages that I had gotten from my birth family would have and did enforce those thoughts of myself. After all, I was worthless, mentally ill with schizophrenia, and suicidal; therefore, in both their eyes and in my own eyes, I did not deserve to breathe my next breath.

Lucky for me, and may I say for all of you out there, Jesus did not feel this way when He went to the cross and took our sins upon Himself for our salvation, if we choose it.

-- -- -- -- -- ✆ -- -- -- -- --

That day? <u>WOW</u>!! <u>What</u> <u>a</u> <u>story</u>!!

In Stone Cold, I wrote what the day before was like, the day before 'That Day!' How Mary spoke to me about Jesus. I told you how that night I had overdosed on sleeping pills, Xanax, and my heart medicines, but I did not go into that long, drawn-out night where time seemed to just standstill. A decade could have fit into a minute and a year into an hour. Mary's words echoed through my head, that either I would be dead or be a Believer by the end of the next day.

I thought that I would show her up and defy her words of death despite overdosing and I knew that I would not become a Believer. However, God and Mary both knew differently, although I'm not sure that Mary knew I would become a Believer, I know that is what she was praying and interceding for. God was leading me, protecting me, and teaching me. Jesus was carrying me and Mary was praying to Jesus and fasting for my deliverance.

Mary spent that whole night standing in the spiritual gap for me in intercessory prayer and fasting. I do not know what she had seen in me, but she saw something excellent and worthy, kind, and pleasant. Mary saw someone who needed a Believer of Jesus to stand in spiritual warfare. Since she was a former Marine, as well as a seasoned Christian, my therapist, and the one who spoke to me straightforwardly and honestly about Jesus, she was not about to walk away from this fight. She had shown me, without my knowledge, the unconditional love

110

that God had revealed to her, and she knew my dirty laundry tales and all.

I, on the other hand, teetered with my own life in the balance, and my eternity lay in the loss or gain of my decision. I was fighting a battle against Satan himself, for he evidently did not want me to win this battle.

The most prolonged hours were from 1:00 am to 3:30 am. The voices were surrounding me ghoulishly and playing with my head. The visual and tactile hallucinations were ominous and fierce, as I kept on popping more and more pills that I had saved for this suicide attempt.

Even though I had taken enough medicine to kill a few elephants, I never got sleepy or felt drugged until the battle was over. It was as if I had popped candy until the moment, I accepted Jesus and went to Mary the next evening. That night I know that God was hanging onto me, Jesus was carrying me, and Mary was praying for me

Father-God did not let Satan defeat my spirit, soul, or even let him have a single hair on my head. I know that there was a sigh of relief in Heaven after the night was over and daybreak was dawning, for the darkness was gone; the Light had won over the dark and all of heaven knew that my soul was going to be saved, for I still had breath in me and the night had passed.

My struggle was still internal, but I did not know this. Yet the heavens knew the choice I would make because the night had passed. Satan was still working a battle tirelessly within the confines of my mind and put me up to challenging God the Father, Himself. I took every gasp of rebellious breath in me and challenged God with the

Casting Crowns song, "Voice of Truth," that Mary had played for me.

When she played it, she explained that God's voice and the voice of Jesus was a "Still Small Voice." The Voice waited patiently for me to listen to it through all the harshness of the crowd, the world, and the demons, and, of course, Satan. She explained that it is in the voice of truth that I would find the love, peace, and comfort that I was longing for; not in death from my own hand. After playing the song for the second time, making me really listen to its words that second time, she said that I can choose to listen to the "Voice of Truth" over those from hell and anguish.

My challenge to God was for Him to play the Casting Crowns song, "Voice of Truth" for me five times in the next four hours. If I won, then I could do with my life as I wanted, live or die when I chose. If He won, I would accept Him as my Abba Father, and Jesus as my Lord, my Savior, and my Big Brother.

I had it all planned out, or so I thought. I was going to make it impossible for Him to play, "Voice of Truth" for me five times in the next six hours, let alone four, just to be safe. Someone forgot to tell me that <u>NOTHING</u> is impossible for God.

That morning, forty-five minutes after making my challenge to God, I had decided that I had already won, for I had not even heard the song for the first time. By the end of the day, I was going to be free to complete my death wish if I choose to. I went to my friend, Chrissy's apartment, where the only radio or media component was an old wall dial antique radio that did not have a plug attached to it. I knew it would be impossible for God to play "Voice of Truth" there.

Suddenly, that old antique radio started to make a static noise. Chrissy and I both walked from her kitchen to the living room where the communication was, and a voice came over the radio, "you've lost, but you've won, you just don't know it yet." Then the "Voice of Truth" played over it. I could not deny that it played because Chrissy, who was NOT a believer, heard it too. I told her my challenge to God, and she accepted Him right then and there, pleading with me to take Him into my life along with her. I was a bit more stubborn than that as that was just once, and much of His time had passed by.

I left Chrissy's and listened to America's Top 10. "Voice of Truth was # 2 and climbing in the charts. Who knew? That was twice in less than 20 minutes. This God figure was catching up fast. I went for a drive, an hour later while I was listening to ASU's radio station, (and ASU is not known for being a Christian University) what should play?!?! You guessed it, "Voice of Truth" by Casting Crowns. The next day there were repercussions for the mistake, but that did not help my situation any. There was now almost an hour and a half left, and by my count, I should have been ahead, but God was leading by a landslide.

I went to see Jeanetta, who is a Hispanic friend of mine and a Believer. She saw that I was bothered, and asked me what was on my mind. Note to self: "Never tell a Believer something that you do not want them to pray about!" She told me that I would not, and could not, win this challenge. Once I left her apartment, she had her church and the whole Campus Crusade for Christ group praying for me. "I was doomed!"

I walked into a local restaurant and heard the song there. Funny, because usually on that day and time of the week, there would often have been someone playing a guitar. On this day, a local DJ happened to be there instead. He was a friend of Jeanetta and knew of me casually through her. Also, being a member of Campus Crusade for Christ, he had received Jeanetta's text message to the Crusade group. He already knew what to play if he was to see me, and he knew how many times I had to hear it in the next 50 minutes.

I left the restaurant because I knew that I was not going to win any challenge there. I went home, where I should have stayed! But, Arthur and Jessica called me over to their house for dinner that evening. They were a young couple who had gotten married after graduation the spring before. Jessica was one of my aides. I figured that I would walk over to their home, which was in a neighborhood north of King Street, where they were renting while attending graduate school. There were only twelve minutes left in my challenge to God, and I now knew that if I were inside, or if I drove, He would win. It seemed logical to me that I could kill time. No car, no building, no radio, I've won, right? Wrong again!

God knows what He is doing when He takes on a challenge. Three minutes left -- I walked next to a car stopped at a light. Their radio was tuned to HIS Radio,

You've got it, "Voice of Truth" was playing. Only three more minutes to go, just three minutes, and my life would have been mine to deal with in the way that I would choose to deal with it; not in having to keep a deal with the Creator in Heaven! He knew that He had it in the bag the whole time.

I cried when I heard "Voice of Truth" for the fifth and final time of the challenge, but God had to play it two more times for me that day. I believe He has a thing for 'sevens.' Three minutes left -- in less than five minutes I knew that I could finish the challenge. I could live or I could die, and there was no God to hold me accountable. But, there is a God, and He proved me wrong, fair and square. If you call playing a song on an antique radio with no plug attached, fair, He won.

Oh, I still doubted and wanted a rebuttal, but I was also afraid of Him at this point. I did not know what He had in mind for me, and that scared the be-gee-bees out of me. I got to Arthur and Jessica's white as a ghost and told them of my last 36 to 48 hours. They praised God, since they had been praying for me for over two years for this day to come. I excused myself from dinner and called the ACT-Team, Mary happened to be on call that Friday night. She met me at my apartment an hour later, we prayed together, and she made sure that I received medical attention for the severe overdose. Just hours after this, my blood pressure dropped to 80/60 and lower, and I was in a different kind of fight.

Through it all, I learned that challenging God is a horrible idea, as He will win the challenge if He takes it

-- -- -- -- -- ✜ -- -- -- -- --

on, or if God doesn't take it on, He may punish you. Rebelling is only futile where He is concerned.

Where it concerns God, even broken things, objects, people, places, or whatever, can be used for His Glory. God can utilize anything, and anyone for His will to be done. Accepting Jesus is probably the most frightening thing I have ever done, but it is also the most rewarding.

I have faltered in my faith many times since praying the sinner's prayer, but He has never once let me go. He fought for me then, and He walks by my side now. In writing my story, or at least the first three chapters of my Christian experience, I have been in constant prayer for each person who reads it. I pray that you will come to terms with life, if it is troubling you, and perhaps that if you do not know God and Jesus as your Savior, you come to know Him now. The sinner's prayer is at the end this book, if you care to say it as I have written it. You may also pray your own version of the prayer. What's important is the state of your heart. There is nothing as invigorating and powerful in this world as coming to Abba Father and Big Brother Jesus as Creator and Lord.

The way my life turned at this point, that in the prior two days I could have easily killed myself, I could have totally turned my back on God, Jesus, and the Holy Spirit. But, God's all-encompassing grace saw me through. He had Mary put it on the line in such a way that I wanted what she had. I just didn't know that I could have it until I truly had it. I went from the darkness of my mental illnesses to the Light of my Savior, Jesus Christ!

-- -- -- -- -- ❧ -- -- -- -- --

Suicide Awareness and Prevention

This section of my book is the most important to me. It is very near and dear to my heart because in my darkest moments of depression, and as I was engulfed in hallucinations and voices from schizophrenia, I had attempted suicide many times.

Because of these attempts, I had coded several times, been pronounced dead, and ended up in ICU with little hope for survival. I now know that Father God has a purpose for my life and kept me here on earth for a reason. He wants me to tell my story so that others may find hope in it. If you or someone you know are experiencing any of the feelings or behaviors that I write about in this section, Please, please find help. The help can be from a friend, family member, a pastor, or professional.

Do not take these signs and symptoms LIGHTLY! By being mindful of them and by getting help before it progresses further, you are doing the right thing. Be caring, understanding, loving, and present in a person's life, you might just save a life.

Many times, what had happened with me could have been avoided with someone just showing that they cared. I had prayed many times that if this person smiles at me or talks to me, I will choose to live. Or, if I get a phone call from someone who wants to talk to me personally, not a sales call, or a robocall, but a call from a friend, yet the call never came. Most of my friends expected me to reach out for them or to them; it never occurred to some

-- -- -- -- -- ❧ -- -- -- -- --

of my friends how badly I had needed them to reach out to me on occasion. I was always the glue that kept our circle of friendship of several friends together, and to them, that was my role. I hungered for one of them to make the move first for a change.

Sometimes, it was because they did not understand. At other times, people just did not want to deal with how sick I had become. Let me tell you from experience, that you should never give up on a person! By reaching out to these people in our life; paying attention to changes in behavior and mood, being there and sticking to a relationship or making friends with someone who is hurting, you may just make a powerful difference and save a life! In doing so, you may be gaining the most special, or closest relationship and friendship of your life. It happened to a couple of my friends.

You may even release the potential of the person to be successful in their lives. Who knows, that person may tell their story, and, in doing so, save countless other lives? You do not know if you are saving the life of one of God's many angels, who happened to get lost for a moment in time.

Please, SEEK HELP!

Wanting to die and to kill themselves,
Feeling hopeless and thinking
They have no reason to live,
Suicide seems to be the answer
For many people feeling like this.

Feeling trapped in emotions
Or in unbearable pain,
And feeling in life,
There is nothing else left to gain.

They sleep too much or too little
And have extreme mood swings.
It's best to seek out help now,
Or, you may regret it one day.

Agitated and Anxious,
May show reckless behavior.
If there are life changes like these,
Please, intervene!
You may just be their life's savior.

Not wanting to be a burden
To loved ones or even to friends,
They may talk about death…

-- -- -- -- -- ⟐ -- -- -- -- --

Don't let them give in!
Drugs and alcohol can be a factor.
So, speak to them please,
And, use some candor.

Seeking revenge, not wanting to forgive
And showing furious rage
Right before or right after
The revenge begins.
If you've waited 'til now,
You had just let them win.

Mental illness can be a factor.
So can past trauma and abuse,
Family history of suicide and prior attempts
Multiply the risk in them.
Do everyone a favor by being mindful of this!

Remind them: they are loved
And cared about by you,
Don't close yourself off to them,
But, please seek out help
And be open and sincere!

-- -- -- -- -- ✑ -- -- -- -- --

Suicide is Forever!
Once you have done it, you have
No More Options! It's The End

Dear Friend,

I know that life gets hard, the road is very bumpy, weary, and all uphill. The rain comes down, and we weather the storms and tragedies of this life. Others are counting on us, and we do not know where the strength will come from to carry ourselves through this life, let alone the ones we love or those who we reach out to help along life's path.

But, we mustn't give up. ___No, not ever!___

The money is short, our loved ones have needs, our neighbor gets sick, and we can use a little help. Dear Lord, how can I do it all alone and still have the strength left to cope?

But, Give-up? *NEVER!*

You get sick, and your life comes to a point where living is a daily battle for health and breath. Both mentally and physically, you want to rest and maybe even quit and throw in the towel because you feel so darn bad all the time. The weight of the universe is on your shoulders, and it seems no one can reach down through the depths of the despair, depression, or darkness to save you. You feel lost and alone. Those little voices inside your head that keep getting bigger, louder, and STRONGER are telling you

-- -- -- -- -- ◆◇ -- -- -- -- --

to do things to yourself, egging you on, "Go ahead; Do it! You know you want to! Couldn't be a better time."

Don't listen to them!
Give-up? ***NO! Not Me!***

Things do get better, and you make new friends. They let you into their families, and you get to celebrate holidays and birthdays with them. You will never feel alone again, believe me, it happens. The fairy tale ending, I am living proof of it if you give yourself permission to go on and not give up as I almost have. There are so many special events in my life that I would have missed altogether. I would have also missed a happy life. One that keeps getting more joyful, and you will miss out too if you commit suicide. Please, Do Not give up!

Please, Don't Ever, Ever Quit
Life Goes On!

Give yourself permission to surf the pain, and then, give yourself permission to LIVE!

Someone out there benefits significantly having you in this world. It would be a tragedy if you were lost to that someone.

Julie Weidner

-- -- -- -- -- ✿ -- -- -- -- --

Suicide Prevention Skills and Statistics

This is a note to tell you of the many skills and strategies learned over several years that have helped me to move through a suicidal mindset episode. I do not in any way stake claim on these skills, I am only saying that they were taught to me and have helped to save my life. I hope that I can reach people in a deep center place of their core being or consciousness where that little spark that still wants to live remains. I know that deep down where everyday struggles collide, this note may bring about a 'light-switch-on' moment. My dream is to help someone hang on long enough that they find happiness somewhere beyond their time of struggle.

Although I cannot assure anyone's happiness -- that will be up to you to find for yourself -- I can assure personal growth in finding a sense of purpose, if you hang on long enough. You will learn that there is always a place in this world that you alone can fill. *No one else can replace you.* These skills and strategies have helped me and many others to come to a place of emotional stability in our lives. I am willing to bet that within a few weeks or a couple of months, with effort on your part, your life will not only be touched by what these skills have taught me, but you will experience a noticeable change for the better.

I have learned that, for me, writing and journaling my feelings is key to getting through a tough moment, especially when I need to talk to someone. But, at that moment there is no one to talk to or no trustworthy person to whom to spill my thoughts, feelings, or deepest emotions. A sheet of paper doesn't reveal your internal struggle with anyone unless you want it to. You can always destroy the paper. In a positive way, destroying it helps to release that negative energy and to bring a more positive state of mind.

Writing is a way of expressing your hurt, pain, and struggle and releasing it to the world so that it doesn't remain solely inside yourself, allowing more positive energy to come in. Writing is also great for noting your victories, successes, fond memories, happy moments, and your blessings. Writing, I have found, is the most viable and useful tool in my toolbox. It is a versatile tool that allows me to release the negative and helps me to absorb the positive.

I had a counselor that taught me to 'surf.' I'm not talking about going to the beach, but about emotions. Let me explain. Have you ever been to the beach or seen it on TV and noticed that the waves end when they come to the shore? Well, a surfer on a surfboard can only ride the wave until it hits the beach. That's right, it comes to an end. The same goes for our struggles, our emotions, our situations, they do eventually end. Some of the waves crash against the beach, and some end gracefully. We just need to swim back out into our ocean of emotions and continue surfing. A positive wave will come along eventually, and if you nurture it, it will build into more and more positive waves, with each wave getting a little higher and bigger, so that they last longer.

If we nurture our positive wave, more likely than not, it will bring along with it more positive waves until your ocean is filled with at least as many positive waves as negative ones. You may even learn to recognize how to avoid the negative waves and to surf mostly the positive waves. Of course, the negative waves will come along out of nowhere, but you will better be able to handle them if you remember that they do end. If you learn how to foster your positive waves, they become the huge waves that you can ride on for what may seem to be the ride of your life. Those waves are rewarding and worth hanging on for. Who knows, you may end up with a treasure chest full of these waves of memories, fulfillment, and happiness.

Breathing is a tool to use also. If you take time to breathe mindfully and skillfully, it can be very uplifting and powerful. By breathing in by two counts less than your breathe out, you physically foster a chemical reaction in your brain that calms you and levels the playing field. Doing this, you allow yourself to think clearer, helping to solve your struggle.

Just by taking deep breaths alone, you allow the positive to resonate within yourself. By concentrating on breathing -- "in the positive and out the negative," -- you are changing your mindset and things seem to get a whole lot more bearable. By doing this type of breathing, you are allowing yourself to internalize positive energies and you in turn add positivity into the universe.

Holding a frozen orange can ground you; it is painful enough to fill a need to feel physical pain. It does not cause permanent damage to your hands or body, but it is a physical grounding tool. I also use holding frozen oranges to ground myself when I am anxious or having

-- -- -- -- -- ✑ -- -- -- -- --

flashbacks. The sensation of the pain brings you into the moment, and the aroma of the citrus smell makes it a pleasurable experience at the same time. It pulls you from the negative thoughts long enough that you can consciously direct your thoughts to a more positive place.

Cooking, washing the dishes, dusting, doing the laundry, or any other chore, fixing the car, building a shed, mowing the lawn, all done in a mindful way, by noticing and participating mentally on every step of what you are doing, is also a useful tool. I will use a couple of these to explain what I mean.

First, we need to know what mindful or mindfully is: it's noticing, participating, and taking in the environment, all your senses, and all that encompasses the moment that you are in and only in that moment. It's like what athletes call being 'in the zone'; or what I call as a writer, my 'magical creative moment.'

When cooking, be mindful of reading the recipe, gathering your ingredients, measuring the ingredients to the recipe's specifications, mixing the ingredients -- first, the dry ingredients, then the wet, then together, noticing the texture of the ingredients. If you are baking bread, notice the elasticity of the dough in your hands as you knead the dough. Notice the cool feel of the dough. Notice how smooth it looks., Notice the feel of the dough on the baking pan along with the flour used to keep it from sticking to the surface. Place it in the oven and, after it bakes, let the aroma of the bread encompass you and take over your imagination. Eat a piece of the bread while it's still warm with the aroma still in the air now residing on your taste buds. Be mindful of your senses, feeling the ingredients, seeing it in every stage of the process of baking from touching the elastic dough, hearing the dough pound on the countertop as you knead the dough, smelling the aroma as it cooks, filling you with desire to dig in and eat it, and the imagination of its taste. Then actually eating the bread and the enjoyment that it all brings.

The same process happens when fixing a car. First, diagnose the problem: there is a flat tire. You diagnosed this problem by sight, probably. You get a spare tire. Both actions are sight-related, because you noticed the flat by looking at the car, and getting a spare, you needed the tire sized properly. Jack the car up, feel the muscles in your body as you lift the lever up and down on the jack. Feel the oil and grime from the old tire and the rubbery feel of the new one.

Having the mind active in doing an activity does not give you a chance of thinking about suicide. What it does is give you something else on which to concentrate.

Listening to music is my favorite pastime when it comes to releasing negative thoughts. I do mean listen, intently and mindfully. Listening to music helps me to feel the emotions that are locked inside that I cannot define or that seem to control me. I find that the song "Let It Go" especially useful for this purpose. I crank up my Amazon Echo and play it as loud as I can without disturbing my neighbors and I 'Let it All Go!'

After all, isn't it the negative, lonely, and difficult moments where life gets into our way, that we are trying to let go? Just hang on in here with me, and I will be praying for you, as I have been while writing this book. I feel that with suicide being in the top ten reasons for death from children nine years old to senior adults, it is my civic responsibility to report some of the rates. Suicide is the second leading cause of death for teenagers in the US and is the third leading cause of death for young adults ages twenty to forty-five years of age; the first leading cause of death is unintentional injury. Suicide is the fourth leading cause of death for adults from forty-five to sixty-four years of age. It remains in the top ten leading causes of death for older adults and is the fourth leading cause of death for children seven to thirteen years old. These statistics are serious, and suicide rates increase every year, with both younger and older people dying.

As someone who has attempted suicide and have found my way out of the suicide cycle, I feel that it is my Christian duty to advise the public of this epidemic. Chances are you currently know someone who is seriously thinking about suicide and you do not even know it. It is even more likely that you know someone who has thought about or has attempted it and are not aware of their struggle to hang on with us. It is my personal story and part of my testimony that suicidal feelings do pass, and that suicide is a permanent solution to a temporary situation, circumstance, or problem.

I was pronounced dead after an attempt. The orderly who was pushing me to the morgue, looked at the doctor, and asked her what he should do with me, after which I sat up, with difficulty breathing. The doctor turned around and passed out when she saw me still alive.

I have had five attempts that I should never have survived: I had friends come over, or missed the paratransit and they called for help, I didn't answer the phone when my Mom called so she called for a wellness check on me. Then there was the attempt that I had made as I challenged God to a duel. I was in ICU for all five of these serious attempts and I attempted again in the hospital. I almost made it during two of these attempts in the hospital, except I had a seizure because of the lack of oxygen getting to my brain. I know personally the struggle of the suicidal spirit taunting, and I can say that fairy tale endings do happen, especially if you fall on your knees and call out to Abba Father, and Jesus.

-- -- -- -- -- ❧ -- -- -- -- --

Suicide Essay Continued

Suicide is becoming more and more prevalent in the world today. Some societies even think that it is honorable. I personally do not know what is honorable about it. It is a desperate plea for help if one is lucky enough to survive a serious attempt and even if a person tries half-heartedly or to gain attention, it is still a cry for help. When a person has an attempt under their belt, the next attempt is more serious and more deadly. At least, I have experienced that myself. Each attempt I had gotten more determined and braver as far as taking my own life.

Please, if you take anything from this book, take that life is precious and so are the people around you. Pay attention to changes and to expressions on strangers' faces. Your smile or words of greeting may just be the catalyst that helps give them strength not to take their own life today, which gives time for them to reconsider, or for God to work a miracle in their life.

Some information that I would like to share with you is the National Suicide Prevention Hotline # 1-800-273-8255.[3]

If you do not believe how serious this crisis is, just think on the fact that suicide is the second highest cause of death for young people today. Do not let someone you know or love become a statistic. It is such a devastation to this world when a suicide happens, but it is an even

---

[3] :https//suicidepreventionlifeline.org

-- -- -- -- -- ❧ -- -- -- -- --

bigger tragedy when it happens because a friend, acquaintance, or loved one looked the other way.

Would you like to receive God's forgiveness?

Yes, we can make it to the Kingdom of Heaven, through Jesus Christ, if we accept Him into our heart.

We cannot earn salvation: we are saved by God's grace when we have faith in his Son, Jesus Christ. All you have to do is confess you are a sinner for whom Christ died, to wash your sin debts away and ask his forgiveness. Then turn from your sins – that's called repentance. Jesus Christ knows you, loves you, and died for you, for all of us. The attitude of your heart, your willingness to serve Him, and your honesty are what is important to Him. It is suggested that you pray the following prayer, accepting Christ as your Lord and Savior.

"Dear Lord Jesus,

I know I am a sinner. I ask your forgiveness, Lord. I believe you were born to die for my sin debt and rose on the third day from the dead. I shall and will trust and follow you as my Lord and Savior. I give my life to you to guard and to guide. Lord, I ask you to help me to do your will in all things. In all things, I worship you, praise you, and give you the glory! In your Holy Name, I pray. Lord, **I pray this sincerely.** *Thank you so very much for my redemption and your love.* Amen*

-- -- -- -- -- ✆ -- -- -- -- --

Now that you have prayed the sinner's prayer, you must attend a healthy church home. Find a loving church that teaches and takes its lessons from the Bible. Have joy in your newfound faith. If you are already a believer, use this time to rededicate your life, and reach out to the lost, help them to come to know Jesus as you do, so that they will meet Him in heaven with you one day.

-- -- -- -- -- ◈ -- -- -- -- --

Thank You

*Thank you, Jesus, for giving me
friends who are true.
Thank you, Jesus, for the Love-light
That comes from them and from You.
Thank you, Jesus, for keeping me alive,
And, Thank you also for my new life.*

Have I Done Things Right?

When the day has come and gone,
And the morning turns to night.
I hope to hold my head up high,
To know I have done things right.

I gave my life to Jesus!
Now I live to glorify Him.
At the end of the day,
And at the end of my life,
I want to see the Love-light in Jesus' eyes
Knowing that He has approved
Of my life as I live it within
My relationship with Him.

-- -- -- -- -- ❦ -- -- -- -- --

Father- God,

I pray tonight, my God, to honor you. May I give glory unto your name, Lord, my Father, Your Majesty! Lord, may my life exemplify the life of Christ, in that others around me can see His love-light stand out through my life. May they see an example in me of how to live with integrity.

Father, I pray for those who are really hurting internally, and are struggling to find a reason to live. Lord, let them find your love and acceptance; to find love and support from those people around them. Thank you, Abba, Father, for their deliverance from the spirit of depression and suicide.

Teach me also, to love and to pray for my enemies. Help me to ask you to bless them, please, Dearest Lord. I'm not talking about financial or material gain, but a blessing that will forever give them gain; that blessing being their acceptance of Jesus Christ so that they can spend eternity with Jesus and You.

Remind me to pray for all those that I love. May they all make it to Heaven above.

Amen

Made in the USA
Columbia, SC
09 September 2020